Many Voices, One Truth

Sifting through Competing Noises that Interfere with the Savior's Voice

By Tracy Taris, MA, LMFT

Copyright © 2022 by Tracy Taris
Soaring Beyond, an imprint of Winged Publications

All rights reserved. Non-commercial interests may reproduce portions of this book without the express written permission of the authors, provided the text does not exceed 500 words.

Commercial interests: No part of this publication may be reproduced in any form, stored in a retrieval system, or transmitted in any form by any means—electronic, photocopy, recording, or otherwise—except as provided by the United States of America copyright law.

Represented by AuthorizeMe Literary Firm,
Sharon Norris Elliott, Agent
PO BOX 1816, South Gate, CA 90280,
www.AuthorizeMe.net   AuthorizeMeNow@gmail.com

All Scripture references from The KJV, ASV, or NIV
© 2011, unless otherwise noted

ISBN: 978-1-956654-83-7

Endorsements:

- As a board-certified clinical neuropsychologist, I've spent decades working with patients to help them understand the importance of our thoughts on our attitudes, beliefs, and behaviors. Learning to discern the origin of the voices we're listening to is key for functioning in the fullness of who God created us to be and utilizing the many gifts He's given us including power, love, and a sound mind. *Many Voices, One Truth* is a valuable resource for all who want to truly filter out the deafening noise of the enemy of our soul to hear God's loving voice above all others.

Dr. Michelle Bengtson

Author of the award-winning book *Breaking Anxiety's Grip: How to Reclaim the Peace God Promises* and host of the award-winning podcast "Your Hope Filled Perspective"

- The quality of our thinking determines the quality of our living. Tracy has assembled an inspiring and practical path to recognize and renew the quality of one's thinking. Becoming aware of the distractions and hindrances to a quality, spiritual life, Tracy equips with a healthy, grounded approach to managing one's inner world which results in a more secure identity and direction. As a Licensed Marriage and Family Therapist and community elder, I strongly recommend this book as an opportunity to grow in some timeless and essential ways.

David Bruce

Licensed Marriage & Family Therapist, Elder

- When I was introduced to the concepts that Tracy teaches, I found myself challenged to reconsider my way of experiencing the presence of God in my life. I had been stuck in an academic way of thinking, which kept God in the box of my interpretation of scripture. Tracy's work introduced me to the notion that the voice of the Holy Spirit could actually speak to me in a way that would harmonize with the Bible and make God's will for me clearer to perceive.

John Steinreich, Church Historian

Author of *A Great Cloud of Witnesses: Lessons for Modern-Day Christians from Church History*

- I have often heard messages from church leaders that discuss how to walk in the will of God, but have not heard many messages about the first step in how to distinguish the voice of God from all others. This is a profound step before you can know what is God's will in the first place. My heart is warmed as my friend and colleague utilizes her three passions: Christianity, counseling, and writing to conceptualize this topic in a way that is authentic and true to her, while making the concept comprehensible for others. As she said, and I concur, that many, even in the church do not know how to take captive thoughts to the pulling down of strong holds over their lives. It is an absolute blessing to have this tool that can extend beyond the therapy room and into the home of others to help uproot the fallible core beliefs that destroy the quality of life of so many individuals. Translating and integrating scriptures with psychological processes is a gift that Tracy demonstrates in her text and brings practical application to aid others in the transforming of their interactions with their thoughts to be empowered to live lives after God's heart.

Summer Richards, MA

Licensed Marriage & Family Therapist

- Many Voices, One Truth does so much more than identify the issue that so many Christians face, which is how to take thoughts captive (we all know this Scripture and it can seem insurmountable). Through Many Voices, One Truth Tracy gives life-changing, practical, and applicable tools that guide us to not only hear the voice of the Savior, but also prompt us to follow His leading!

I have known Tracy's work as a Marriage and Family Therapist for many years. She has helped countless people to live in the freedom that is promised in Christ and her personal and professional experiences are reflected in this book. Many Voices, One Truth is a must read for anyone looking to declutter their mind and walk in a connected relationship with The Savior.

Sandi Derby

Advanced Grief Recovery Specialist®, Speaker

Author of *Living Born Again, The Uncomfortable Journey*

- All of us struggle with the messages that we receive from our life experiences, interactions with others, and spiritual battles. In Many Voices, One Truth, experienced counselor Tracy Taris, LMFT, combines a deep understanding of life development, brain science, and coping skills with God's truth creating a powerful tool for life change.

Michelle Nietert, M.A., LPC-S

Author of *Loved and Cherished, Make Up Your Mind,* and *God, I Feel Sad*, YourMentalHealthCoach.com

Foreword

"The gatekeeper opens the gate for him, and the sheep listen to his voice. He calls his own sheep by name and leads them out. When he has brought out all his own, he goes on ahead of them, and his sheep follow him because they know his voice. But they will never follow a stranger; in fact, they will run away from him because they do not recognize a stranger's voice."

John 10:3-5.

Every week, in one form or another, I am asked by a spiritual seeker, "But how do I know if what I am hearing really is from God and not just my imagination?"

This question most often surfaces in an experiential, spiritual renewal, and transformation training course I facilitate. Tracy Taris not only attended the course for herself but also hosted it in her home for neighbors and friends. In the course we move from focusing on performance and results, to focusing on becoming the kind of people God intended us to be. We learn ways to let go of the tiring and disappointing task of expecting our efforts and hard work to change our hearts. Instead, we engage with God in community for refreshment, renewal and transformation. We deepen our intimacy with God, learn to hear the Spirit and welcome Him as the primary agent of change in our lives.

The series Tracy hosted was the last in-person course conducted before the Covid pandemic prohibited group gatherings in our area. Since then, the course has been offered online, where thirsty souls from Manila to Johannesburg and from Los Angeles to London have learned to discern the movements of the Spirit within them.

When asked why I offer the classes free of charge I adapted the words of a poem to convey my intentions.

"My intention is to discern the activity of God around me and participate with Him as He demonstrates that everything flowers from within, though sometimes it is necessary to reteach a thing its loveliness, to put a hand on it and retell it in words and in touch that it is lovely, until it flowers again from within."

Tracy Taris is a kindred spirit, and I knew I had a treasure in my hands from the first chapter of *Many Voices, One Truth: Sifting Through Competing Noise that Interferes with the Savior's Voice.*

My mind immediately began to fill with all the ways that Tracy's four channels example would so clearly and convincingly help participants in my course discern God's voice from any other. It clicked immediately for me when she compared listening to the voices of Self, Satan, Society or the Savior to tuning into the old TV channels I grew up watching: ABC, CBS, NBC, and PBS.

But when she talked about some of us being "still tuned in to phantom images" from programs that "went out of syndication a long time ago," something shifted in me. I felt it viscerally. It was like old thoughts and images I had carried for years were officially canceled right on the spot.

It felt like Tracy was directly speaking to me when she wrote, "Don't abdicate your emotional energy to someone else's indignation." So powerfully true! Where was this book 30 years ago?

It is said that master teachers are known for conveying deep truths in simple stories. The stories told in "Many Voices, One Truth", and the analogies offered are familiar and accessible.

The wisdom and examples brought forth in "Many Voices, One Truth" were hewed from Tracy's relentless pursuit of God's presence. And when not garnered from her personal experience she is able to call upon years of clinical practice where the presence and the power of God are manifested in the work she does.

"Many Voices, One Truth" offers practicals for three important foundations in living a Spirit-led life. First of all, it answers the question, "Where should I direct my attention if I want to hear from God?" Second, "How do I discern God's voice from any competing voices?" And third, "What do I do with what I have heard?"

The quality, depth, and breadth of "Many Voices, One Truth," is no surprise to me. I have known Tracy for nearly

20 years and have seen her live a Spirit-led life by discerning the voice of God.

I first met Tracy in the early 2000s when our families where in the same small group in La Canada, California. Her devotion to God and passion for life were evident to everyone who met her. Tracy's love for others, defense of the marginalized, and fierce advocacy for what is right and true shines forth just as brightly.

Tracy Taris is a trail blazer. She is a woman of great faith in God and passion for others. For decades she has been a stalwart advocate for greater intimacy with God and a lifestyle imbued with rhythms of attention to the Spirit. She has marked a path of spirituality in a religious tradition largely bereft of attending to the immediate presence of God.

Tracy was among a handful of brave souls who would regularly meet together with senior leadership to explore ways for members in the fellowship to more diligently attune to the Spirit and surrender to His leading.

In "Many Voices, One Truth," Tracy proclaims boldly the full life available for us in Christ. But where this book excels beyond many is that Tracy also provides step-by-step directions on how to get there and a picture of what it will look and feel like when you get there.

An essay I wrote on soul care was published a couple months ago. One of the last things requested of me by the editor was to provide 2-3 book recommendations to readers for further study. I wish I had already read "Many Voices, One Truth." It would have been tops on my list.

You owe it to yourself to get a copy of "Many Voices, One Truth" today.

- **Byron Parson,** Author of *Walk This Way: The Spirit-Led Life*

Acknowledgments

I'd like to thank my Lord and Savior Jesus Christ whose belief in me helps me to hold on to the truth of who He says I am. Your love for me, Lord, is what drives me to show others the way to Your heart and to the Word You've provided for us. I know You will be with each and every individual who takes the time to read this book. Draw them ever closer to You, Lord.

I'd like to thank my husband, Michael Taris, whose dedication to me and our family encourages me to pursue my dream of writing and to pursue my dream of helping others hear from and believe God. Michael, your commitment to your own creativity inspires me to give time to that part of myself. Your ability to see God in music, and to see music in pretty much everything in life, has spurred me on to look at the bright side, to search for truth, and to honor the Holy Spirit when He calls me to create.

I'd like to thank my daughter, Lexi, whose gentleness in spirit is a soothing balm for our whole family. Lexi, you are one of the best moms I know, even though you're so new at it. I admire your ability to be patient with yourself and with others. Thank you for bringing our grandbaby into our lives. Autumn, Duchess would like to thank you for simply existing.

I'd like to thank my daughter Jazmine, who inspires me

with the way she fearlessly stands in and lives her truth. Jazmine, you are wise beyond your years. I admire your ability to stand up for yourself and for others and your ability be your own person. Your dedication to doing things well is an inspiration to our whole family.

My daughters, I am proud of you for who you are and who you are becoming.

I'd like to thank every woman who has ever been in a small Bible study group with me, and who has encouraged me to make time for writing whenever I complained I didn't have time. Your collective words of wisdom held me up when I couldn't do it for myself.

Finally, I'd like to thank everyone who buys this book either for themself or for someone they love. May you grow in your capacity to tune in to the voice of Jesus; may you believe all He has for you; and may you become all He created you to be.

Peace be with you,
Tracy

Dedication:

This work is dedicated to my daughter, Jazmine, who overcame the battle with negative thinking patterns and whose experience was the catalyst that spurred me on to complete this book. Jazmine, may the voice of the Lord Jesus Christ always guide how you see yourself and others. Love, Mom.

Table of Contents

Part One: The Voices
Page 1

Chapter One: Where Does Listening Come From?
Page 2

Chapter Two: May We Have Your Attention Please?
Page 13

Chapter Three: Competing Voice #1 – Self
Page 30

Chapter Four: Competing Voice #2 – Satan
Page 44

Chapter Five: Competing Voice #3 – Society
Page 68

Chapter Six: Competing Voice #4 – Savior
Page 86

<u>Part Two: Static Interference</u>
Page 106

Chapter Seven: Hindrance #1 – Relational Sin
Page 107

Chapter Eight: Hindrance #2 – Shame
Page 119

Chapter Nine: Hindrance #3 – Distraction
Page 130

Chapter Ten: Hindrance #4 – Fear
Page 159

<u>Part Three: The Strengthened (Soaring) Identity</u>
Page 170

Chapter Eleven: Be Still and Know that He is God: Tools to Stay Tuned-In to The Savior's Voice
Page 171

Chapter Twelve: Illustration of a Tuned-In Life
Page 191

Part One:
The Voices

Chapter One

Where does "Listening" Come From?

A Reckoning

As I stood mesmerized by the bubbles on the surface of boiling red spaghetti sauce, I wasn't prepared for the life challenge that was on its way through the telephone line.

"Hello." As soon as the word was out, the tension emanating through the line caused my body to stiffen in fear.

"Tracy," the voice said and paused before continuing. Some part of my brain was taking in the rest of the message, but the room and sounds around me blurred and slowed to a crawl. The sound of blood pounding in my ears was the most prominent reminder that I had not died on the spot.

I vaguely heard my husband, Michael, ask, "Sweetie, what's wrong?"

His words seemed to be coming from under water. *Is that Michael talking?* I looked over. He was staring at me, concern furrowing his brow, waiting for an answer.

Hot tears stung my eyes as the words escaped my mouth. "Tut had a stroke."

According to the voice on the phone, Tut, my younger sister whose real name is Tangelina, was in stable condition. Still, I knew I had to go be with her. I had to leave—like the next day.

Our small group at church was having Bible study that night at our house. I didn't want to conceal the disaster from them, so I used the evening to lean into my church family to pray for my sister, my family, and for me. Michael and I didn't have the money for a last-minute flight, so our friends, Mike and Mary, paid for my trip. In fact, Mary pulled out her phone and asked me when I wanted to leave for Houston and return to Los Angeles. She booked a round-trip flight right on the spot.

Upon arriving in Houston, I met up with three of our sisters, and we discovered that Tut, because of her young age, had handled the stroke remarkably well. She was young and resilient, and with the proper treatment and pertinent life changes, she would recover from the stroke a lot faster than most people who experience a stroke later in life. This news was a relief, but we were all still grief-stricken.

Grief is a finicky emotion. How it is experienced can

largely be based on what you already think of it. For my sisters and me, we each dealt with our grief in different ways. Two of us faced the sadness head-on and allowed ourselves to feel it immediately. One sister distracted herself with things that didn't seem to have anything to do with what was going on in the moment, and one dove into the necessities that needed to be taken care of on Tut's behalf.

Being a marriage and family therapist (psychotherapist), you'd think I would have been one of the two who faced the grief head-on and allowed myself to feel and to be in the moment, but that wasn't the case. I chose to dive into what needed to be taken care of. At this point in my career journey, as an intern, I had worked with families in need of connection to community services. I took it upon myself to work with the hospital social workers to put care in place for Tut once my other three sisters and I had returned to California. What that meant was signing her up for things like unemployment, disability benefits, etc.

My other sisters each chose their own way of handling their grief. What I learned from my choice was that at unimaginably difficult times, I tend to work my way through without taking a pause to process what's going on or go to God for guidance or consolation.

Because I was working to deflect my grief, it was difficult handling the social services tasks at hand, and much internal frustration and fear ensued. While standing in line at one agency after another, I began to feel guilty because I also felt tired, scared, and homesick. I ignored this because Tut needed someone to stand in the gap for her by setting up these services while she was still in the hospital.

I was completely open to these tasks, but something kept needling the back of my mind, making me want to escape. At first, I thought it was fatigue from the busyness of the phone calls, driving around an unfamiliar town, and standing in long lines, but the ache in my heart felt deeper than exhaustion. It wouldn't go away until I sat with it to figure out what was going on internally. Reflecting on all that was happening brought up a memory from my past.

My mother had once traced a line on the palm of my hand with her index finger and told me I had a short lifeline. She then declared I would die young, and she would be devastated. I was about six years old at the time, so I was the one who was devastated. I believed her. I believed one day I would devastate my mother by dying young. Tut's stroke and brush with death brought up for me a fear I'd always had of dying young. During the time of helping my sister, this fear began to work to get the best of me on an unconscious level. Deep down I wanted to return home to my husband and children and not think about death. I felt selfish for having these thoughts and feelings and for wanting to escape.

One of my sisters, who chose to respond to the grief by allowing herself to feel it, leaned into the sadness while having a small spiritual crisis at the same time. She didn't understand why God would allow our sister to have a stroke, and she was angry with Him. I resonated with her on some level but was afraid to admit it. Her expression of her thoughts and feelings prompted me to ask myself what I believed about God's goodness. I also started wondering what I believed about myself. For some reason, out of nowhere, feelings of suicide surfaced.

Digging Deep

I called Martha, a close friend, but one whom I had not had that much contact with in the previous few years. Our lives had taken us in different directions, but I had a distinct impression that it was she whom I should call. Martha and I were once roommates, so she knew my story and some of my family history. I told her what was happening and how I was feeling about it all, including my current suicidal feelings.

There is a difference between suicidal *thoughts*, which can involve plans or thoughts of how to carry out the act, and suicidal *feelings* which involve feelings of unworthiness and hopelessness. My feelings were the latter.

Martha listened patiently and then gave her assessment. "Tracy, this has nothing to do with what is currently going on. It has to do with what you believe about yourself."

Martha went on to summarize aspects of the story I'd

just given her, hitting on the key point that was driving my angst—what I believed about myself. Her comments reminded me of Isaiah 41:10 where the Lord commands us not to fear and to remember (think about the fact) that He is my God who will help me. This applied both to the fear I had regarding my sister's health and to fears for my own life. In working through all of the case management and setting up my sister for when I was going to go back home, I was distracting myself from the belief planted by my mother that I would die young. The distraction of setting up services gave me a momentary reprieve from an old belief brought on by my sister's stroke. Missing my family, feeling under duress, and wanting to go home made me desire an escape and a return to safety, when what I thought I should have desired was to continue doing what my sister needed. All of this prompted thoughts that I was nothing but a selfish person.

When Martha assessed that the sadness and suicidality had more to do with what I believed about myself, she was talking about material from my childhood. In my childhood, one of my aunts told me I was evil from a very young age.

I remember eating a bag of potato chips at four years old. One of my cousins looked into my bag, and I moved it away from him, asking him not to look into my bag. The aunt, who gave me the message that I was evil, snatched the bag away from me, gave me a mean look, and handed it to him. My cousin smiled and dumped his handful of chips into my bag. I hadn't noticed he didn't have a bag of chips, that he had only a handful. But I was punished for being evil and selfish.

Over time, hearing the evil/selfish message over and over, I internalized this as true and feared it most of my life. After all, I was taught that evil people go to hell. I was told countless times until I left home at eighteen that I was going to "burn in hell!" I'm not sure when I started believing it, but I'm sure it was from a very young age. At any rate, my brain eventually created a neuropathway of belief so deep it took years of much prayer, fasting, and psychotherapy to change my thinking. It also took people who loved me, who insisted I was not evil, and who pointed out examples and proof to redirect those neuropathways to more accurate, life-giving beliefs about who I was and who God created me to be.

Here I was now, an adult, a follower of Jesus for many years, and the brunt of the misdirected childhood belief had come full force. I had spent much time in therapy and in scripture working to uproot the old, implanted, inaccurate belief, but on a level deep, deep down, I still believed what I had been told about myself. The Holy Spirit used the incident of my sister's stroke and my subsequent rolling up my sleeves to help her, to dredge up from the depths of my soul that which needed to be discarded in order for me to move forward as a spiritually healthy woman of God.

Though I'd addressed the false belief previously, I wasn't, however, aware of the resentment I harbored toward myself because of the agreement I made with my aunt long ago that I was evil, selfish, no good, and hell bound. I came to believe, after speaking with Martha, that God was calling me to deal with this deeply ingrained core issue once and for all.

I was about to complete the training process that would allow me to become a licensed psychotherapist. When I got the call about my sister's stroke, I had just passed my first exam. I was due to take the second and final exam before the year was out. Once my licensing process was complete, I planned to open a private practice. Entering into this new stage in my life, I could no longer allow the deep belief that I was an evil person to have a place. How would I be able to help my clients process their own pain and erroneous beliefs?

I thought I had fully processed my own pain and incorrect beliefs through therapy and through being Jesus' disciple—discovering His truth and holding onto it. Many times I had told myself that I'd no longer believed myself to be evil. Yes, I had submitted to the Holy Spirit for healing, but sometimes, healing has to run deep for it to be eradicated.

This is especially true for wounds inflicted by words from people in one's family-of-origin, especially one's primary caregivers. So, I didn't spend years hiding from pain. On the contrary, I'd spent a good bit of the last fifteen years or so dealing with it. But, as Jesus said in Matthew 17:21, "this one can only come out by prayer and fasting," sometimes you have to bring out the big guns.

The Power of Belief

Belief, as a follower of Jesus Christ, is one of the biggest guns in your arsenal. Prayer and other weapons in our arsenal often activate belief when it is lacking. Fasting brings us to a place of soul submission whereby we present our soul before the throne of Christ, or in some cases at the foot of the cross, humbled and in desperate need of the petition we are requesting.

We can fool our conscious mind some of the time, but we can't fool our unconscious mind any of the time. If there is a belief we hold, we can tell ourself we've moved on, but the unconscious will hold it in until we excavate it out and it's really gone. Or, we can process material that upholds a belief, as I did. But, if the rabbit hole is deeper, we have to get in there to root out the belief and challenge it with truth. Our unconscious mind will constantly give us clues through dreams, words we say, and behaviors we do. The infamous, "I don't know why I said/did that" comment is often an indication that we *do* know why. We just aren't aware that we know.

For healing to take place, material locked away in the unconscious must come forward. Until you do something about the unconscious material by either changing it or accepting it to start living in congruence with it, there will always be triggers that throw you for a loop. Acceptance of a lie and choosing to live with it as if it is true is sometimes one of the excuses people use to engage in bad or harmful behavior. What they have chosen to believe is what they have been told all their life: *This is what they think I am, so this is what I'll be.* Tragic.

So many people live in the image of man instead of in the image of God who created them. So many people live out a story someone else wrote for them instead of finding out who they were created to be. They never live their intended life.

Just as you can choose to believe something, you can also choose to stop believing it. You can replace an erroneous belief with truth or an alternate way of perceiving the situation. Unbelieving something and replacing it with truth takes practice, and that practice can become a skill. Through this book, I intend to show you exactly how to incorporate this skill into your life.

When I went through the time of my sister's stroke, the thoughts that popped into my mind were not about the beliefs that I was evil, selfish, and going to hell themselves. What I went through was more about what voices I was allowing into my mind. More importantly, the experience was about God and me because what I believe about myself is ultimately what I believe about Him.

A.W. Tozer coined it this way, "The most portentous fact about any man is not what he at a given time may say or do, but what he in his deep heart conceives God to be like. We tend by a secret law of the soul to move toward our mental image of God." (1)

The contents of this book will help you confront beliefs you hold about yourself that contradict what God's Word says. You will learn to replace incorrect beliefs about yourself with what the Word of God says about who you actually are.

I use the metaphor of voices to show how a person has a constant barrage of thoughts that originate from one of four different sources: the voice of Self, the voice of Satan, the voice of Society, and the voice of our Savior. Think through, pray through, and apply the lessons you learn. By doing so, you will come to grasp the power of God's Word, the power of believing—really believing—that as His follower, you are a new creation. If you are not yet His follower, my hope is for you to identify what has been holding you back from Him. You may think you're held back from God because of *organized religion* or *hypocritical people*, but what's really holding you back is what you believe about yourself.

At the end of the day, you are who God says you are, and you are what His Word says you are. It is possible to turn away from self-deprecating beliefs you gathered throughout your life, no matter where they originated from—Self, Satan, or Society and turn to the Savior.

Chapter Two

May We Have Your Attention Please?

When I was growing up there were only three major television networks. They even referred to themselves as "The Big Three." They were ABC, the American Broadcasting Channel; NBC, the National Broadcasting Channel; and CBS (formerly) the Columbia Broadcasting System. If you were watching anything at all on television, you were probably tuned in to one of these three major channels. A less-than-popular fourth network was the Public Broadcasting Service or PBS. These networks broadcasted their messages or programming and competed for viewer attention.

Incoming thoughts operate in much the same manner as far as what we give our attention to. When we watched television back then, we were almost certainly tuned in to one of those four voices: ABC, NBC, CBS, or PBS. Your mind operates in much the same way, especially during times of leisure, worry, or work. Your mind is almost constantly on a channel. Here we will talk about four different channels.

Spiritually and mentally speaking, there are four major broadcast voices: Self, Satan, Society, and Savior. You know which voice you're on at any given moment primarily by the content that is broadcast to you—to your heart. The Bible says, "Every good and every perfect gift is from above" (James 1:17 [KJV]). Let's use this reference as it pertains to your thoughts.

If your mind is peaceful, stable, content, and in a place of gratitude and love, then you are tuned into the voice of the Savior.

If your mind is filled with turmoil, fear, disgust, hate, and lies about yourself and those you love, you are tuned into the voice of Satan.

If your mind is filled with discontent, competition, or envy, you are tuned into Society's voice.

If, in the moment, you are relying on positive beliefs about yourself that have been sent to you by loving family members, peers, or, by your own positive experiences, you may be tuned into the Self channel, which by the grace of God can be an affiliate of the Savior's channel. Conversely, if your mind is filled with worry, uncertainty, insecurity, or criticism, you can also be tuned into your very own broadcasting voice, which at times can be an affiliate of Satan's voice or Society's voice.

Unlike the Savior's or Satan's voice, the voices from Self and Society can broadcast both positive and negative messages. However, Society and Self can be influenced by the first two. The Savior's and Satan's voices do not influence each other. What has light to do with dark (2 Corinthians 6:14)? And what does Christ have to do with Belial (2 Corinthians 6:15)?

Operation from the Self voice depends, in the moment, on what has been poured into you or on what memories you are tuned in to at the moment. Regarding positive or negative influences, most people operate by default more in one than the other.

Applying the interventions you will learn here will show you how to tap into God's voice. You will also learn how to allow the positive messages and beliefs from your childhood and current life to have some airtime. My overarching hope is that you will then pay more heed to what God has to say and let Him also influence the Self voice's thoughts.

Let's say we refer to listening to God as the positive side. In psychology, we call listening to and operating from the positive side of the Self's voice "high or good self-esteem," but it's really a compilation of what has been poured into you by God and by the affirming people and experiences He places in your life. On the other hand, listening to and operating from the negative side of the Self voice is called "low self-esteem" because the messages are coming from negative beliefs within yourself about yourself. Make no mistake, they were originally placed there by unhealthy people in your life whom Satan used. This is the way the process works:

- You hear a message or experience a situation ("You can't do anything right!")
- You have a thought about that message/situation ("My mom thinks I'm stupid.")
- You make an agreement with that thought ("I must be stupid.")
- You develop a belief which operates in the background of your consciousness making difficult circumstances seem insurmountable when they really aren't. You come to believe they are undefeatable because of what you believe about yourself.

You made agreements with these messages, and they

may still be operating in your life. At any rate, because no one ever came along to correct these messages, you were left at some point to your own defenses and interpreted the messages, which eventually became negative tapes looping endlessly within your mind.

If there is one thing you learn about these destructive broadcasts, know this: Satan may not always be at the helm of your negative thoughts 24/7. You can be trained into thought patterns that assure you will never see yourself as God intended, and you will never see yourself for who you really are. The training can go so well that Satan can use his resources elsewhere to torment others. God is the only Being who is omnipresent, meaning He is in all places, all at once. Satan, and his minions, are created beings and can only be in one place at a time. It makes perfect economic sense for him to spread his resources and budget them out. I fully believe there are times he'll tell a minion, "She's got this, so go over there and torture the soul in apartment 4B."

But just as with television channels and the selection of broadcasts, you can change the voice anytime you want. God has even given you tools and authority in Jesus' name to do just that. Don't be hypnotized by the images on the screen of your mind. Many of those images, as you will see in some of the exercises here, went out of syndication a long time ago. But, you're still tuned in to phantom images—living your life through a soap opera or drama that hasn't had a new line or new actors in years.

Tuning In to True Belief

Though I no longer believed I was an evil person, my lack of turning to scripture and believing what God said about me prevented the replacement of negative beliefs. The truth is, I am His creation and He loves His creation. I'd done a lot of work to heal and to accept God's love. For the most part, it helped. I'd identified negative thoughts and beliefs that I knew were not true. I'd accepted my responsibility for my reaction to hurtful life situations, events, and experiences, and I'd begun to hold onto what 2 Corinthians 5:17 says about people in Christ being new creations. For the most part, I had begun to believe.

Being a new creation often comes with surrounding yourself with new people. Most of the people in my new life in Christ were life-affirming, encouraging, interested in who I was as a person, and interested in my growth and their own. They also had enough love for me to reproach me when things weren't right. When they saw sin or selfishness playing out in my behavior, they spoke up.

The broadcast voices still served up a daily playlist, but I learned how to manage the channels and turn some up, down, or off. However, some of the beliefs I grew up with remained deep down in the circuitry of my brain and in the recesses of my soul. They lay there dormant, waiting to use a hurtful interaction as an opportunity to present themselves. In the case of my sister's stroke, I began to feel guilty because the belief that I was evil surfaced from my unconscious mind once I determined I wanted to get back to my own life.

In addition to being evil, I apparently had "ugly ways." When Tina McElroy Ansa wrote a book by the same title, (1) I wondered if it was more than a familial expression. I felt sad about being called evil. I didn't want to be evil or have "ugly ways," but I had been conditioned by a process called "limbic imprinting." *Limbic imprinting* is a process that happens in our brain from birth until we are about seven years old when we take in information indiscriminately. (2) Imprinting in the brain's limbic system creates the emotional map of deeply ingrained beliefs and values that govern our behaviors on an unconscious level. From birth to about five-to-seven years old, most of the information coming to us is from our parents or other adults who are important for our care. Many of our thoughts, behaviors, and beliefs are stored in our subconscious and unconscious mind.

Imprinting continues until we are about thirteen, but from about seven to thirteen-years old, we also begin *modeling* the behavior of the adults around us. (3) Before the age of seven, we take in information, whether positive or negative, without question. We don't think through whether or not it's true. That means, everything positive we are told we accept as true. Everything negative we are told we accept as true as well. Whatever we are told, whatever we witness in our innocence, we take in without any kind of analysis of whatever else is going on at the time.

Around early adolescence, the beliefs we've gathered are locked in. Illustratively, our brain stores them much like positive (+) signs or negative (-) signs. (See illustration below).

When new information comes in, the brain looks for a match. If we are told the positive message, "You are a good person," but that positive finds nothing to match it in its file of beliefs about ourself, we reject this. By the same token, if told "You are dumb," and if that negative finds no match, the brain will reject this as well. It's not a matter of rejecting positive and accepting negatives, which is what most people suffering with self-esteem issues do, it's a matter of finding matches that can be built upon.

What Belief Does This Match?

From the ages of thirteen to twenty-one years old, the *modeling* process continues in a form of observational learning. Changes in behaving, ways of thinking, and ways of emoting come from watching or observing other people's behaviors or the consequences of their behaviors, and repeating the same. These repeating behaviors become agreements which eventually become ingrained beliefs.

The way out of the snare produced by unconscious agreements and beliefs is to identify them when they are occurring and use tools to change the negatives to positives. This is not done by using positive psychology but by using truth. Jesus didn't say positivity will set you free, as modern psychology would have you believe. Jesus very matter-of-factly stated, "The truth will set you free" (John 8:31-32).

One of the jobs of a type of psychotherapy, called cognitive therapy, is to identify the negative beliefs, find a truth within the situation, and replace the negative belief with truth. The way it works is to identify the negative belief, where it came from, and find another truthful way of viewing the situation that could turn the belief into something more acceptable.

Again, we are not talking about positive thinking. It is more about finding out what is true or what is a different perspective to which you can adhere.

To an extent and for a short while, you can trick yourself into believing something positive, but it rarely lasts unless you truly come to believe it. Repeating positive mantras do not last unless the mantra becomes true. Truth has a mystique no one can touch. There isn't anything you can do to change truth. It is what it is. A positive declaration doesn't cease to be true just because a large number of people no longer believe it. And a lie doesn't become true just because a large number of people say it is so. A lie is a lie; the truth is the truth. People telling themselves and others lies are still simply telling lies.

You see, when there's a cultural agenda, a belief that Society's voice wants you to adopt, it's constantly in your face through the media, forums, coffee shops, college and university classrooms, etc. The drivers of the agenda push it, not because they want you to believe it, but because they are most often, unconsciously, trying to convince themselves. There is a collective unconscious thought that says, "If I—or *we* because there is such a thing as a collective unconscious—can convince enough people to believe this, maybe I (we) will too. Then I (we) won't see it as wrong. I (we) can finally do what I (we) want without anyone telling me (us) it isn't right." This deceitful game goes on in the minds of many. Trickery is one of the ways people try to silence their conscious mind from telling them the truth against whatever lie they are pushing or whatever deed they want to do.

Memory Sorting

Our unconscious mind has the job of storing and organizing memories. Since this is such a big job, the unconscious mind will often take the path of least resistance. Whatever behaviors, beliefs, or information it is exposed to repeatedly, the unconscious mind adopts.

When new, incoming information shows up, the unconscious mind searches for a match. As already stated, if you are constantly told you do not matter, negative experiences are accepted as truth.

For example, let's say you're in your middle school physical education class. The P.E. teacher selects two captains to choose teams for volleyball. The two captains take turns picking your peers to be on their team, but no one picks you. Because of the negative imprint, "I don't matter," already in your mind, being skipped over for the volleyball team finds a match. You further accept the *fact* that because you were not picked, you do not matter. If the teacher does not notice you weren't chosen, your belief that you do not matter is compounded. Your unconscious mind accepts as fact the negative imprint that you do not matter.

If you were to bring up in therapy that you've always felt you did not matter, I would explore this belief by asking when you first felt that way, or by engaging you in a discussion of life stories that demonstrated that you did not matter.

Let's say the volleyball story came up. I would listen with the purpose of allowing you to process pain around the event, as well as to allow me to conceptualize how you internalized your experience. I would need to know what your unconscious mind may have done to give meaning to the experience. Then I would use therapeutic tools to help you learn how to challenge your negative thoughts. In our work together, you should be able to pick apart the volleyball story and find an alternate meaning that may also be true.

For instance, you realize that you'd forgotten that you were sitting on the far edge of the bleachers while everyone else was standing in a cluster waiting to be chosen. You'd also forgotten that the P.E. teacher was distracted that day and had handed over responsibility for the class to the two captains. He'd immediately walked off for an important call in his office. Neither the captains nor he noticed you were sitting on the edge, and you'd done nothing to make yourself known. Why would you if you felt you didn't matter?

In discussing forgotten elements of the story, you may be able to come up with a different meaning like, "I wasn't chosen because the two captains didn't see me, and everyone was anxious to start the game. Plus, both teams had the nine players needed to make up a team, so why would they notice me? In addition, the P.E. teacher seemed to have a lot on his mind, and he'd often trusted the two captains he chose that day to take leadership of the class."

In this new reflection on the situation, you can possibly have your first experience with challenging the "I don't matter" belief. Repeated unpacking of different stories from your life helps you understand yourself better. You begin to implement the skills of questioning what you believe in the moment, identifying the meaning you are giving to it, and finding an alternate truth. Through current or in some cases past experiences, you slowly begin to erode the belief that you do not matter.

Again, this isn't about positive thinking. There's a lot of research on positive thinking, and I won't go into it here. But for the purpose of what we are trying to accomplish—which is understanding belief—the important thing would be for you to identify what else is or could be true about the situation you are challenging.

On the positive side, let's say you've been told your whole life you are smart. Your unconscious mind will flat-out reject some experience that comes to you in your adult years to tell you that you are dumb. For example, I have a cousin whose father always called her a dumb blonde. For years, that label haunted her and debilitated her academic endeavors. She believed she was too dumb to tackle the difficult concepts in math, so she couldn't finish her degree. My cousin avoided taking math in college and would drop out once she was on a roll with accumulating credits. She'd always give herself a reasonable, well-thought-out excuse to drop out. Though the reasons seemed valid each time she came up with them, deep down they were rooted in her belief that she was too dumb to finish anyway.

Years later, when I'd developed a deep relationship with her and her family, her dad would call me dumb, or he would say something else that communicated the things he was used to saying to her. They had absolutely no effect on me.

One day she said to me, "How do you do it? The things my dad says to you would floor me, but they don't have any impact on you whatsoever!"

I simply said, "Because he's not my dad. He's crazy if he thinks I'm dumb."

And I really believed it was *his* problem, not mine. There was nothing in me that connected to what he was saying to make me feel anything I wasn't. In other words, because I'd always known or believed—not just felt—I was capable academically, I had always been a good student who received praise for my efforts from teachers, peers, report cards, and returned assignments, so deep down I knew I was smart. Deep down, anyone telling me otherwise, didn't fit my view of myself or my capabilities. When the criticism or statement that I was dumb came, it didn't find a match, so my unconscious mind rejected it. But when my cousin's father said the exact same thing to her, a match for the idea was already set up in her mind and heart, so she accepted his comment as true and often chose debilitating behaviors accordingly.

Discerning the Voices

What you do with incoming information tells you what voice is currently broadcasting in your mind. With the P.E. class example, the channel is either from Satan or Self because of how the situation made you feel in the moment. You weren't uplifted. You didn't feel loved. You believed you were less than the other students. And you probably still feel the same way as you recall the story. In the dumb-blonde story, the channel was Self. I didn't feel anything negative about myself in regard to my intelligence because the dumb comment didn't match any of my experiences about myself. I knew who I was regardless of the message given to me in the moment.

Had I had already implanted thoughts like, "You have everything you need in Christ," or "You are fearfully and wonderfully made," I would have known the Savior's channel was broadcasting. I wasn't tuned into the Word enough at that time to hear God's messages although they were being broadcast at the time. Having scriptures come to mind to confirm the truth happens once we have the Word deep down inside us. The Holy Spirit can then remind us of what we know to be true of God—we can then hear the voice of God. Sometimes the Spirit will use scripture directly and sometimes He will simply whisper a truth we know but we may not be thinking of in the moment.

When incoming information is received, the unconscious mind will identify it as positive or negative, look for a match, then either accept or reject it. This is done in milliseconds. I never felt any animosity toward my uncle. Whatever he said to me didn't hurt, as it would my cousin, because there was no match. My belief was the opposite, so my mind didn't accept the information or color my view of myself, nor my view of him. He's awesome as an uncle. One of my favorites, hands down. He even gave me away at my wedding. But because I didn't already believe about myself what he was saying, my mind rejected his words.

Someone else's words or behavior registering as some kind of emotional tweak is an important clue as you learn this process of knowing how to regulate what you believe. The things that hurt are often indicators of what you already believe, though you don't always consciously know you believe it. On the surface, it may seem that the person who said the hurtful comment is being an insensitive jerk, but the truth is, something in what they have said is attached to something you already believe.

At times, people are just plain cruel or inconsiderate. Some of the things they say may hurt momentarily. Often, we can shake those words off rather quickly and go on with our day. We won't even think about what was said unless someone else brings it up. However, when the hurt remains for days and weeks, we need to pay attention—we need to check our beliefs. Some signs that we need belief-reassessment are if we *relive* the experience. We may rehearse over and over what we should have said. Or we may continually calculate how we'll handle the next similar encounter with that person. If any of these reactions takes place, a negative pre-programmed match has probably been sparked. Figuring it out is your first step to freedom. Changing it is the second step.

The next four chapters will cover how to recognize the four different broadcast voices.

Chapter Three

Competing Voice #1 Self

"In the beginning God created the heaven and the earth...and God said, 'Let there be light:' and there was light. And God saw the light, that it was good: and God divided the light from the darkness" (Genesis 1:1, 3-4 [KJV]). Genesis goes on to discuss all the other things God created, and after each daily session of creating, "God saw that it was good."

Likewise, when we do something and feel we've done a good job, we are pleased, right? Well, so was God. He was pleased with the things He was making. The end of the first chapter of Genesis leads up to the pinnacle of creation: Man. God felt He was doing such a good job He decided to make man in His own image. "And God said, 'Let us make man in our image, after our likeness: and let them have dominion…over the birds of the heavens…and over all the earth, and over every creeping thing…' And God created man in His own image, in the image of God created He him; male and female created He them" (Genesis 1:26-27 [ASV]). God said to Himself that this was good, *very good* in fact (v 31, italics added).

One of the reasons God created us is because it pleased Him to do so. God didn't necessarily *need* us. He created us because He *wanted* us. It pleased Him to create us in His image. Being image bearers mean many things. An image reflects, as when you look in a mirror or in any reflective surface. You see a reflection of yourself. One of the definitions of reflection is, "a thing that is a consequence of or arises from something else." We are the consequence of God's creativity; we arise from Him. We are from God. We are made to bear His likeness. Because of sin, whether our sins, others' sins toward us, or sin's mere presence in the world (Genesis 4:7), we have been deterred from our original state—that of being made in the image of the Father, Son, and Holy Spirit.

Part of our spiritual journey is the task of getting back to God our Father, who made us in His image. But the journey is also a journey to return to our original self, to that person God had in mind when He created us individually.

John Bunyan's classic tale, *The Pilgrim's Progress*, is an allegory of the Christian soul as it journeys through life. (1) Bunyan wrote the story while he was imprisoned for conducting religious service outside the Church of England. Thus, one of the principal themes in the book is the struggle for freedom. Christian, the hero of the tale, has to traverse many obstacles in his path to reach his destination. From a psychospiritual standpoint, where he is going is home, to his True Self. We all construct a journey toward the False Self to survive the unbearable, like not feeling loved or wanted.

The False Self

Dr. Donald Winnicott was a psychoanalyst who first coined the phrase "False Self" to describe the side of ourselves we create in order to protect the inner, more vulnerable True Self. (2) Even in healthy parent-child relationships, the False Self can develop as a way to protect the inner person. However much the False Self has protected us, operating for too long from that side of ourselves can cause all kinds of mental, emotional, and relational ailments.

To be able to walk in, operate from, and be the person God had in mind when He created you is a magnificent freedom in which to dwell.

In His Image or In My Parents' Image?

When God made us, He had a particular someone in mind. He knew what He was doing. Then He gave us to our parents. Experiences with them or some other significant-adult force in our life started reshaping us into their image.

Psychologist Erik Erikson mapped out distinct psychosocial developmental stages that every person must go through. (3) When navigated well, we reach adulthood looking pretty much like what God had in mind. Unfortunately, because all of our parents are human, no matter how good or well-adjusted they were, we learn how to construct a False Self. Some of it seems built-in, since one of the ways we learn about life is by modeling what we see. Therefore, some of what we see, both good and not-so-good, can become a replica of what we've witnessed.

If our psychosocial development is merely an issue of modeling, a relatively healthy person will at some point, usually during adolescence, start to discover their own way of doing things and perceiving the world. Unfortunately, some of us never find our own identity and end up becoming more like our parents than we would care to admit. Some parents even demand, both consciously and unconsciously, that we follow in their footsteps.

The messages we receive about who we are expected to be are most often communicated nonverbally. During the fifth stage of psychosocial development—Identity vs. Role Confusion—the task is to figure out who we are apart from who our parents say we are. Guess what age range this covers? If you guessed adolescence, you guessed right. Most parents see the teenage years as a time of rebellion. The teen years often become a rebellious season, not so much because the teenagers are in "a rebellious stage," but because of their parents' response to whatever they are doing or not doing.

Differentiation

In the "who am I besides who my parents say I am" stage, teenagers are going through the process of differentiation. Differentiation does not mean separation. Separation means cutting oneself off from the family. Separation isn't necessarily healthy because God created us for relationship. Differentiation is a discovery process. In it we learn how to tell the difference between our experience of life and the experiences of people around us. (4)

For example, with differentiation, if you are celebrating Thanksgiving with your extended family, and your dad and his father do not get along, when the feast is over, you are able to connect to the good and uplifting interactions that occurred during the visit, even (and maybe especially) those with your grandfather.

If you are not differentiated, you may feel angry because of an argument your dad had with your grandfather. The argument may not have had anything to do with you. It may not even be an argument that others were aware of, but because you have not yet differentiated, the seething hostility Dad may feel because Granddad took the last roll—"and he knew I wanted it," and all that—you may leave the gathering with an underlying sense of hostility yourself. You may even "hate family holidays," if that is your father's experience or mantra after a family gathering.

But in actuality, you do not hate it. You enjoy it. You may not enjoy Dad's complaints about it on the drive home or in the days to come, and if you are differentiated, you are able to tell the difference. For example, "I love holiday gathering with my extended family members. My dad does not, and that's okay. However, I don't enjoy Dad's pouting over this or that slight as the next few days pass." With differentiation, you don't necessarily judge Dad or Granddad—well, if you're still a teenager you probably do—but the point is, you are able to tell the difference between your experience of something and someone else's experience.

Intrapsychic Differentiation

Another form of differentiation is intrapsychic differentiation, which is the ability to tell the difference between a thought and a feeling. (5) In my work with people who come in for therapy, often one of the first interventions I have to use is teaching people how to distinguish between the two. Here's a quick tip: If someone asks you how you feel about something and you name an emotion word, that's a feeling. If your answer comes out in a phrase, sentence, or a paragraph, those are thoughts about whatever you've been asked.

This is important because no matter how close or disconnected your family is, no matter how nurturing or abusive your parents are, you are created to be you. You may look like your parents, but you are your own person with your own temperament—your own needs and wants. You have your own dreams and ambitions.

All your components were carefully chosen by your Father in heaven. He knew what He was doing, and there is no flaw in His design. If you can trade out some of the negative core beliefs you have about yourself for the idea that you are your own person, it will help you have a healthier self-image as well as open your heart to believing God more than you believe the negative thoughts that assault your mind.

Our patterns of belief recreate us into our own image or into the image of those around us. We end up reflecting the sum of what others say about us or what we think they believe. So, what we think about ourselves fluctuates along with the ever-changing views of our culture. If it's cool or hip to do or be this or that, we end up saying that cool or hip thing about ourselves, and that's what we end up naming as our beliefs. Anxieties and/or depression can manifest because of the constant state of flux in which we find ourselves.

We were originally made in truth, and we are to live truth that does not fluctuate to match the whims of society. Our living outside of who we are meant to be will always cause a sense of being ill-at-ease within our frame of mind or sense of self.

Choosing What to Believe

In his book, *As a Man Thinketh*, writer James Allen wrote that man is the sum total of his thoughts. (6) Our thoughts are the sum total of what we believe. As human beings, we get to decide what we believe and what we do not believe, though many of us are either not aware of this or do not take advantage of this fact enough by putting it into practice. Making decisions about our beliefs must be practiced as a daily endeavor because the sum of our beliefs is developed over time. How we tend to think is formed as a result of experiences spanning from early life (some say from as early as the womb), up to our present day. Our pattern is our usual way of thinking—our default train of thought which can be negative or positive as stated in the discussion of the four voices. Again, the Self Voice can either be an affiliate of God's Voice, Satan's voice, or your own habitual way of thinking about events and life situations.

Ephesians 6:10-20 talks about the influence demons can have in our lives. Verse 12 says, "For our wrestling is not against flesh and blood, but against the principalities, against the powers, against the world-rulers of this darkness, against the spiritual host of wickedness in the heavenly places" (ASV). Most Bible scholars will say this is about the spiritual battle for our souls, and based on my understanding of that passage, other Bible passages about the subject, and research I've done, I believe they are correct. But I'd like to pose a hypothesis. What if we looked at Ephesians 6:10-20 from a psycho-spiritual perspective?

Many people who come in for therapy are really coming in to take off layers they sense do not belong. I find it interesting, as a marriage and family therapist, that right before God talks about the spiritual battle, He talks about what our relationships should look like. The verses right before the passage about the spiritual battle in Ephesians 6:1-9 talk about relationships and how they are to be conducted. Children are to obey and honor their parents. Fathers are told to nurture their children and be sure not to provoke them. Workers are admonished to work for their employers as if they were working for Christ.

Therapy is a relational field. In fact, a portion of our scope of practice is defined as, "The practice of marriage, family, and child counseling shall mean that service performed with individual, couples, or groups wherein interpersonal relationships are examined for the purpose of achieving more adequate, satisfying, and productive marriage and family adjustments." (7) Even the world acknowledges that the origin of dysfunction comes from a relational basis and healing comes from a relationship base.

Now, let's hypothesize that the reason those particular directives on relationships are right before the verses on the spiritual battle is because relationship issues are points of entry where those spiritual battles often begin. Having established that, could it be that it is in relationships that one begins to believe false things about oneself or that false beliefs are confirmed? Could it be that if a young woman were to drift away from the truth of herself, could she be susceptible to negative beliefs about herself? Could she drift into a belief pattern that is miles away from who she is created to be? Could she drift into her False Self?

In my work with clients in therapy, I have come to learn that just as we have three states of consciousness—the conscious mind, sub-conscious, and the unconscious—there is often an underlying reason in each state of consciousness when a person presents with a problem. Take for example the eating disorder of anorexia nervosa in which the person starves herself by refusing to eat. A conscious (or surface/obvious) reason may be a belief that she is not thin enough due to comparing herself to what she sees on television or at school. A subconscious reason may be an internal drive for perfection. And an unconscious reason may be fear of not being loved.

If Ephesian 6:1-9—the part of the Scripture that speaks about relationships within the family—is correct and the girl's family functioned in opposition to the directive, we could find that all three levels, conscious, subconscious, and unconscious reasons behind the anorexia, may have resulted from a dysfunctional family system. Simply put, maybe her anorexia is due to everyone ignoring everyone else.

Or perhaps there was some act of dysfunction within the family system, say an alcoholic father. Father would be drunk and beat up Mom if the house and kids were not in order when he got home from work. In putting this together in early childhood, the oldest daughter who later develops anorexia, starts helping her mother get the house and the siblings in order so that Dad doesn't have a reason to get mad. As she grows it becomes more and more difficult to keep things in order, not because she's not doing it well enough—although she soon starts to believe the lie "I'm not good enough"— but because her father's drunkenness worsens over time.

As time continues, she attempts to control her life and the lives of those around her. Because control in and of itself is an illusion, she starts to feel out of control and develops a nagging fear that she just can't place. Eventually, this may lead to something she feels she can control—her eating. At first, she thinks she just wants to be skinny, like the other girls at school. It seems reasonable enough, right? But is it really about the other girls? She thinks so, until the illness gets out of hand or begins to threaten her health.

When she goes to therapy and presents her story, the therapist may assess that comparisons have triggered the disordered eating behaviors. As she and the therapist work together, they discover that the girl tends to feel intense anxiety when she feels things are out of place.

This leads to the subconscious reason for anorexia. She strives to force the out-of-place into place, just like she did when she helped her mom, only she is not aware that she is just repeating the same plot through a different story and different characters. When she sees that no matter what she does, she still feels the same inside even when she starves herself and loses weight, it's not enough to make that feeling—that need for perfection—go away.

In her therapy process, she can work on accepting the fact that nothing and no one is perfect. She may even start to feel better, and the disordered eating behaviors may even subside. But, until she gets to that unconscious belief—the one that says she is not worthy of love, the one that says she has to work for love and make things perfect or be perfect—she will never be at peace. At least not for long. Until that lie is transformed into truth, she will always be susceptible.

Unfortunately, most therapy terminates at the subconscious understanding of what feeds the behavior that is making the person's life unmanageable. Some even stop at the surface level because work at any of these levels brings relief. Jesus said the truth will set you free. In our example, it isn't that the girl is comparing herself or striving to be perfect. Yes, she is doing those things, but comparison and perfection are symptoms of the deepest truth. The core truth is that because she had a father who beat up her mother and yelled at her and her siblings, she doesn't feel worthy of love. So, the striving for the perfect body is actually grief for the love she never had. She could have had love at one time, but Dad's drinking behaviors led him down a path that caused him to exhibit unloving behaviors that ultimately negatively impacted his daughter's view of herself. This example underscores the point of Ephesians 6:1-9. If there is harmony within the family system, the chances of having to fight the darkness of a spiritual battle, whether initiated in the spirit realm or the realm of lies you've told yourself, is greatly diminished.

In giving directives about what family life should look like, could it be that God is pointing to the idea that the door opens to issues of abandonment, rejection, humiliation, injustice, and betrayal when relationships are off? Psychology refers to these emotions as "soul wounds." They are often the entry point to depression, anxiety, self-esteem and self-doubt issues. (8) When a person is bound up in resentment, anger, bitterness, and unforgiveness, she can often feel as if the feelings take on a life of their own.

Looking at Ephesians 6 from a psycho-spiritual perspective, we can see that the truth of God's Word can bring healing. The girl in the example cannot travel back in time to life as a child in her family of origin. Although, when people grow up and reenact the same dynamics from their childhood, they are doing time travel in that they recreate what they formerly knew in their current lives.

Jesus came so we can have abundant life (John

10:10). His intent in creating us was not for us to have a life of sorrows. Although He had many sorrows (Isaiah 53:3), and although He said we would have sorrow (John 16:33), Jesus' sorrow stemmed from many things. One is because of sin in the world. I believe another reason for Jesus's sorrow is because we have forgotten the truth of who we are—we are children of the Living God, Creator of the Universe. Read on for practical understanding and application of the Word that will teach you how to tune into this truth and make it part of your new way of thinking.

Chapter Four

Competing Voice #2 – Satan

First and foremost, Satan's voice, or what he has to say to you, will always contradict or twist God's Word. Sometimes it's subtle. The third chapter in Genesis begins with "Now the serpent was more crafty ("more subtle," KJV) than any of the wild animals the Lord God had made. He said to the woman, "Did God really say, 'You must not eat from any tree in the garden?'" As a psychotherapist, my job is to interpret what is going on relationally between two people, or to assess the inner turmoil a person can engage in within herself. Looking at the exchange between Eve and Satan through my therapist lens, it seems that this conversation picks up on a dialogue already in progress.

Twisting The Truth

Whatever Eve had said to Satan prior to 3:1, he subtly distorted for the purpose of twisting God's Word. Satan is cunning, to be sure. He isn't omniscient. When his voice is coming through, it may start with something subtle, to find out where you are in your own thoughts so he can assess how far he can move you away from the Savior's voice.

Most scholars believe Eve to have been completely innocent, since God told Adam, not Eve, not to eat from the tree of knowledge of good and evil. Apparently, Adam passed the command on to her for she knew to correct Satan when he twisted God's words about not eating from any tree. Satan asked her if God had really said she mustn't eat from *any* tree. Eve corrected him by saying they were allowed to eat from the trees with the exception of one and that they shouldn't touch it, or they would die. Whether she added the words, "you must not touch it" to highlight what God had said, or whether she added that because Adam told her God said not to touch it, the result is the same. She ended up doing the very thing God had told Adam they should not do.

What I want you to learn from this lesson on Satan's voice is the fact that you can choose who you will believe. God told them not to eat the fruit. Satan told them to eat the fruit and they would gain something good—wisdom. Since the fall, we have a tendency to engage with Satan rather than resist, as James 4:7 says.

Though Eve was innocent in this exchange because the fall had not yet occurred, today we aren't always innocent when we decide to engage in thoughts from Satan's network. Satan's invasion of your mind won't always come in the form of tearing you down. Sometimes it will be a temptation. If it is a temptation, you aren't listening to the Savior's voice. God doesn't tempt people (James 1:13).

Sometimes Satan uses the truth to lie to you, but he'll twist it to trap you and entangle your mind. On some level, Eve may have been attracted to the tree and curious about the fruit, which is normal. Satan took a normal thought and deceived her into thinking she wasn't already what God said she was. God had created Adam and Eve in His own likeness. He gave of His likeness freely. Satan said they needed to do something *more* to be like God. To this day many of us are doing the same thing. God says we are loved, valued, and wanted. We believe we have to do something *more* to prove or earn our value.

Further into the conversation, Satan did more than *twist* God's Word. He outright negated what God said by stating in 3:4, "You will not surely die." This happens on a daily basis. God's Word tells us one thing, Satan whispers another, and we go with what Satan says instead of what God says.

Putting the Interaction Together

Regarding this interaction, understand this: After the fall, we play a part in our own deception by entertaining thoughts Satan brings to our mind. As human beings, we have the capability of controlling what we will or will not think about. Thoughts that contradict what God has told you about yourself should be interrupted immediately, preferably with a truth from scripture. At least stop the thought by challenging it with what you know to be true.

Therapists and psychologists use techniques from Cognitive-Behavioral Therapy (CBT). *Cognitive* refers to your thoughts. *Behavioral* refers to the behaviors you engage in as a result of those thoughts. Some of the tools I will show you have their basis in CBT as well as contemplative prayer practices.

The main idea behind the use of CBT is to *choose* to think something else. The idea behind contemplative prayer, for the purpose of the included exercises, is not only to still your mind, but to also still your very self. Be mindful of your thoughts. Become aware of what you are choosing to believe. Quiet your soul. These activities will help you learn to tune into God's voice.

When I was a child, there was a public service announcement on television about the value of education. It stated, "The mind is a terrible thing to waste." God gave us a mind for thinking, yet many people abdicate the throne of their mind. They don't use it to think. They allow it to be carried along, to drift here and there.

Our mind is the main battlefield where Satan uses his strategies against us. He will always put in our mind that he has more control over us than he actually has. In fact, he has no control over us. Not even God pulls that card. God has given us free will and He doesn't override it. Satan, on the other hand, tries to convince us to believe he can override our free will. He can't.

When it seems as if Satan overrides our free will, it is because we have given up our rights. How do we do this? Through belief and through agreement. Every person walking the planet has faith. This is exhibited when people believe what Satan says—hook, line, and sinker. Most people who struggle with faith aren't struggling with belief. They have no problem believing Satan, yet doubting what God says seems to come with little or no effort.

This is most apparent when it comes to what God says about us as humans. God says we are created in His image (Genesis 1:27); Satan says we are worthless or not good enough. People will believe they're not good enough much more quickly than they will believe they are made in God's image. Satan tells people they are not qualified; First Peter 2:9 says we are a chosen race and a royal priesthood. You may believe you are alone, but God says He will never leave you nor forsake you (Deuteronomy 31:6 and Hebrews 13:5). Deep down you may believe you are no good as a person, but God looked at everything He made—including you—and saw that it was "very good" (Genesis 1:31).

The Trickster

While Satan began by being subtle with Eve, there are times when he is not so subtle. I once had a friend who was in love with a man at her church. She told me what a godly man he was. She gushed about how gentle and sweet he was, and how he made her feel like a princess, the daughter of the King, which, of course, she was—the daughter of our Father the King. He was doing a service to her by helping her to live in that truth. He helped her debunk the lies she'd often been told about herself and her worth. She discussed how her new boyfriend honored God and worked hard for the kingdom of Christ. Just as I was beginning to celebrate my friend's good blessing, she said, "He just has to figure out how to leave his wife."

Wait! Hold up! What? I think I used those three phrases in rapid-fire succession. "He's married?"

"Yes, but he doesn't love her, and she doesn't inspire his love for God. She doesn't believe in his dreams, and she holds him back from his kingdom potential."

"But you guys are committing adultery," I said.

"How do you know I'm sleeping with him?" she shot accusingly. "Don't be judging me!"

"I wasn't even thinking about your sleeping with him." For whatever reason, I was only thinking she was involved in an emotional affair. "You're telling me you are having a relationship with him. Of course, you shouldn't be sleeping with him, but you shouldn't be having any kind of intimate interactions with him at all.

Are you sleeping with him?"

Silence. Then. "You have no right to judge me."

This was intended to shut me down, and I'm ashamed now to say that it did. I didn't say anything more on the subject. I thought a lot about it, but I didn't know what to do. If I'd had the maturity I developed over the last twenty five years, I would have continued the conversation by saying something like, "I'm not judging you. The Bible clearly states, 'Thou shalt not commit adultery.'" I would have explained to my friend that she was in an adulterous relationship, and I would have challenged her to repent of her actions and confess them to God and to someone in her church.

But I didn't. And I always regretted it. What I didn't know at the time was the words "you're judging me" are powerful and are often used as a weapon to shut down legitimate righteous indignation. Judgment is one thing and, in some cases, shouldn't be engaged in. But the Bible states that we are to hold each other accountable. Galatians 6:1a says if we see one of our own, a brother or sister in Christ sin, we should gently say something to them about it. That's different from judgment.

Judging and holding someone accountable are two very different things. As brothers and sisters in Christ, our responsibility to each other is to help each other stay on the narrow path toward eternal life. We are to speak, act, and live our lives remembering that we will be judged with mercy by the law of liberty (James 2:1-13). Being reminded of what the Bible says about an issue or circumstance we're in does not constitute judgment. If we feel judged, it's because God's Word is doing the judging. We're responsible for obeying it, not making excuses to get around it.

Judgment Versus Observation

Fear of being labeled judgmental has created a stain on our culture and on society in general. It has created a political correctness that halts truth in its tracks. Once we've been labeled judgmental, we back down, even when we shouldn't. All in all, it prevents people from standing up for what is right. Let me take a few minutes to point out a distinction.

There is a clear difference between judgment and observation. If you are telling me that you are in a relationship with a married man, I am observing a piece of your life that you are sharing with me. If I see you out at a restaurant cuddled up with someone I know to be a married man, and I call you out on it, I am observing your behavior, not judging you. If you tell me you've been working closely at church on a program with someone of the opposite sex and you *sound* to me as if or *act* as if you are smitten by this person, and I jump to the conclusion that you are having an affair with him, then I am judging you. I'm deducing based on conclusions worked through in my own head. In other words, you're not telling me you're having an affair, and I'm not seeing any evidence. I'm inferring probably based on my own experience or filters that have nothing to do with you.

Learn how to tell the difference, and don't back down from standing up for righteousness when someone throws out an accusation that you are judging them. If someone accuses you of being hateful because you disagree on the grounds of what God's Word says as a way to end the conversation, stand up for what you believe. As well if someone accuses you of being judgmental as a way of interrupting their own conscience that may lead to conviction and repentance on their part, stand up for what you believe. Go back to what the issue really is and don't get distracted by allowing the person to bait you into making it about you.

When did believing God become equated with hate or bigotry? Charlton Heston, an actor from the 1940s through the 90s stated, "Political Correctness is tyranny with manners." (1) He was correct.

In order to reverse this, people of God have to learn how to become comfortable enough in who they are to reject something that doesn't fit. If the shoe fits and you are doing something for which you need to repent, you have to do something about it. But, if the shoe doesn't fit, don't wear the label and say so. For example, if someone says, "You're a bigot," or "you are hateful," stand up for the truth and respond, "I am not hateful; I am merely stating that what you say you are doing, or what I see you doing, is not right."

People are usually well aware they are in sin. My friend may have been trying to use me as an affirmation to silence her conscience about dallying with this married man. But in my response that she was wrong, she may have felt some prickles playing around the edges of her conscience, casting doubt on her belief that she was in the right because "he wasn't happy with his wife" or because his wife "didn't inspire his love for God." She was silencing her own conscience and deflecting those whispers by accusing me, using a phrase that worked at the time. Who wants to be judgmental, right? Well at twenty-seven, I certainly did not want to be seen as judgmental, but at fifty-three, I don't wear ill-fitting shoes anymore. Don't wait that long, dear reader. Learn how to speak the truth in love and stand your ground for what is right.

Cues that the Voice You Hear Is from Satan

Satan will always lead you away from God's commands. "Thou shalt not commit adultery" is clear, no matter how unhappy the married person is in their situation. "Thou shalt not…" means "Do not do…," or as my grandmother would say, "You'd bed (better) not…!"

God is not the author of confusion (1 Corinthians 14:33), but Satan is a being of confusion. By the way, never refer to him as opposite of God because he isn't. That would make him equal to God. God has no equal and He has no opposite. Satan is a created being who chose to disobey God and fell as a result. End of story.

He has power, to be sure, because he is also an eternal being and a fallen angel. But he has no power *over* us. He can hurt us, yes, but most of the power he has, we give it to him. Guess how? Again, through our *beliefs* or *internal agreements* and our *behavior* based on those beliefs and agreements.

When Satan speaks to you, there is no peace, only anxiety and confusion. Where there is confusion, there is no clarity, at least not that we can see. Where thoughts are concerned, when there is anxiety, Satan is certainly on the task. Even if there is someone helping you by pointing the way to clarity, if anxiety is onboard, Satan is right there, distorting clarity. One way to test the voice is to think about the decision. Does it bring a sense of peace or anxiety? If you're anxious, the decision isn't from God. God doesn't just *have* peace or *promote* peace, He *is* peace. "The Lord Is Peace" (Judges 6:24).

There are times when you can't connect to the idea that the decision feels right. Just because you can't see the outcome doesn't mean you don't have peace about it. If the decision is from God, you'll feel settled about it. You may not want to obey it, but there is a feeling of being settled on some level, and you'll know it to be right. You may not even understand why you're not more upset than you think you should be. If you have a desire to learn to hear God's voice, if you are willing to change in your level of relationship with God, and if you act on what you know to be right, then the ability to be in tune with God's voice grows.

MANY VOICES, ONE TRUTH

Here are some attributes of Satan's voice:

1. He rushes you – Satan is like a used car salesman in a shiny suit or one of those commercials that scream at you to "act now" in order to get the best deal you can. This rushing tactic is part of the bullying process, but it's also designed to prevent you from thinking things through. Rushing is designed to coerce you to act impulsively. With this tactic, Satan encourages you to make the decision without praying about it or running it by someone you trust.

2. He frightens you – "If you don't do this, then this will happen." The choice will come across as it's something you have to ward off or run away from instead of one that is guided by clear thought and conviction.

3. He makes you obsess or worries you – Like a gnat that won't go away, you can't stop thinking about it. You're just bothered. Your thoughts turn to worry in an obsessive way: "Do it." "Make the move." "Right now," and so on.

4. He condemns you – When people need to make decisions, they have to engage in the process of weighing and thinking, which are internal exercises about the external issues they are pondering. Penalizing you for taking the time to reflect will cause you to make a less than stellar choice. Satan tries to make you feel condemned for engaging in the thinking

process, or he tries to stress you out through fear or a barrage of thoughts that condemn you.

When the devil attacks, he accuses. Satan is called the accuser because that's the meaning of the word Satan and because accusation is a huge part of his makeup (Revelation 12:10). When you have thoughts that you are never going to change, you're not good enough, or you're useless and evil, do you feel good about these thoughts? Sometimes you feel like you will never amount to anything of worth. Satan lives to foster doubt—doubt about God, doubt about goodness, doubt about you and the ones who love you. Most of all, his job is to foster doubt about your worth. He knows who you really are, and that scares him.

When Satan's attacks are successful, they debilitate you, because you have forgotten who you really are. You've forgotten your real name. You are made in the image of the Almighty God. God's voice affirms who you are even when His Spirit is convicting you of sin. He is gently reaching out in mercy even when He has to point to something that needs changing in your heart that for your sake, you need to make. He knows who He's created you to be. God believes in you because He's the one who designed you. Sin is like a virus that causes a flaw in the design, so He sent His Son to redeem you.

Our current culture doesn't like the word *sin*. It is often one of the words people will use to throw you off track and accuse you of judging them. No, we shouldn't go around pointing out people's sin—that's God's job to bring them to conviction. He may use you to do that, as He was trying to do with me and my friend who was dating the married man. In the culture we live in, people just want to do what they want to do. That's what free will is all about—being able to choose between doing what you want to do, or what God is calling you to do.

When you fail—when you make a choice that is against God's will—that's what Jesus' death is all about. He came to redeem us from sin and the death that sin ultimately brings. I'm not just talking about the death of the physical body at the end of your life. I'm talking about the death of your spirit, your sense of self.

I believe the reason so many people love to watch zombie movies and television shows like *The Walking Dead* is because they can relate to them. There are many people who are *the walking dead*. They have breath and blood coursing through their system, but they are by no means really living. They are walking around, relating, working, eating, sleeping, but they are dead inside. On this side of eternity, that kind of death is the real consequence of living a life filled with sin.

Redeeming Your Thought Life

Redemption isn't just about eternity. Redemption helps you get back on track, back to who God originally designed when He made you. Satan has no interest in redemption. He will lie to you about who you are and pound it into the neuro-circuitry of your brain (and your belief system) until the groove is so deep, it's almost impossible to root out. Satan wants to make it almost impossible to get back to who you were created to be. And most of the time he almost can. Almost, but not quite.

If you stop believing what Satan says and start believing what Christ says, you'll be well on your way to escaping the enemy's clutches. Satan is a liar, the father of lies, actually (John 8:44). He was the first one to tell a lie back in Genesis with the whole "you will surely not die" thing. Once someone tells a lie and it is believed by the hearer, love and trust are broken. When Satan lied to Eve, and she let the lie in, her trust in God was broken. When we listen to what Satan tells us about ourselves, we question who we are, our purpose, our legitimacy, our worth, and our value. When he lies about someone we love, we question that person. We question their love for us, we question who they say they are as a person, and we question their legitimacy.

You may be thinking of someone in your life about whom you have believed a lie, but can you see how this is true of God as well? If God says in His Word that He is one thing, you are one thing, and He feels thus and so about you, but Satan tells you otherwise, who do you question? God. You may even see evidence of God's love and being in other people's lives, but you can't see that evidence in yours. You can't see it, but it is there.

Your sight is compromised by the lies you are allowing to infiltrate and settle into your mind as truth. Before long, you, as a believer, *may* believe that God is who He says He is. He's just not those wonderful things for you.

Disentangling the Problem

It's a heart-wrenching problem. In my practice, I've seen countless people who suffer needless anguish because of lies Satan has told them, and that they've adopted as truth. I've seen him do this in marriages. Nine times out of ten, when couples come in for therapy, they are often both saying they want the same from the other person, or they are both blaming the other one for the same thing. What is happening? They are questioning the legitimacy of the person with whom they loved enough to marry.

A wife may be coming in for counseling because her husband doesn't spend time with her. The husband may be coming in for therapy because his wife nags him all the time. Each will name the efforts they are contributing to solve the problem, but they can't see the chicken and egg factor of the predicament—which came first: the nagging or the pulling away?

At the end of the day, they both desire to be with each other, but they can't see their way out of the fog. Often the answer is to get them to see the conundrum and make a commitment to start working on the solution. In marriage, whenever there is conflict, the wife is not the problem, and the husband is not the problem, but the problem is the problem. The key is to find out what needs to be done about the problem itself instead of pointing fingers at one another. My goal is to get them to protect each other and the relationship. I use the analogy of drawing their swords to fight back-to-back whatever is harming their relationship, instead of fighting one another. This is often a tough intervention to pull off.

Because Satan is a being of confusion, the havoc he's been wreaking on a marriage has the couple mired in a bog by the time they come in for therapy. Again, it may seem impossible to turn around, but it's not. Healing in marriage and other relationships often begins with a change in perspective. The couple needs to be open to seeing the relationship in a different way and have a willingness to stop questioning the legitimacy of their partner's love for them. Oftentimes, way down deep, they need to stop questioning the legitimacy of who they are and the fact that they deserve to be in a happy marriage. Most problems, when whittled down, will come to what a person believes about themselves.

I have a hypothesis that one of Satan's high-ranking minions is called *Root Spirit*. The job of this creature is to convince humankind that they are misled about where they come from, and who they are. Root will tell you opposite things about yourself. In fact, whatever it is you are struggling with is probably the exact place you are being attacked because it is the exact place God designed for you to be.

If you are called to preach or evangelize to bring people to God, or if you're called to heal, teach, or counsel to help people grow in their faith, Root will try to stop you. He will lie to you and tell you that you have nothing good to say, that people will laugh at you, that you will not make any sense.

If you are called to be a stay-at-home mom, Root will tell you that you're a terrible mother, maybe that you shouldn't have even had children. Every time you yell at your kids or speak in an impatient manner, Root will tell you that you shouldn't be around those kids, that you will ruin them. If you are called to be a writer, Root will tell you that you are too busy to sit down and write. He will tell you that you have no talent or your writing doesn't make sense.

Root will tell you that you need to be perfect to get anything done. This promotes perfectionism which promotes anxiety. We live in a fallen world, and all of us are just trying to figure out life one step at a time. In Matthew 5:48, Jesus says, "Be perfect, therefore, as your heavenly Father is perfect" (NIV). Some Christians interpret this to mean perfect as in sinless. Since Romans 3:23 says, everyone has sinned and fallen short of God's glory, Jesus couldn't have meant be perfect as in sinless because then the Bible would contradict itself.

The word *perfect*, in this verse, comes from the Greek word *teleios*, which according to *Strong's Concordance* means: 1: complete in all its parts, 2: full grown, full of age, and, 3: especially to the completeness of Christian character. Greek philosophers used the word teleios, or perfect, to mean something being in its *intended function*. In other words, what Jesus was really saying in Matthew 5:48 is to be who God created or *intended* you to be—created in His image (Genesis 1:27), and the purpose of life's journey as a Christ follower is to be transformed into His likeness (2 Corinthians 3:18), and that you are predestined to be conformed to His likeness (Romans 8:29). You were created through God's good and perfect will. Sin caused the fall. Transformation is needed to return back to your originally intended design.

Turning your attention back to the Spirit of Root and the idea of perfection, if you do something well, and are almost perfect because of talent bestowed upon you by God, and because of diligence, Root will tell you that you are not perfect. Not only that, he will tell you that you should be, but that you are far from it. He will tell you perfection for you isn't even attainable, even though you are considered by your peers to be the best in your field.

Most people will believe Root, not the success they receive as evidence and not the opinions of the peers they respect. Root is a sly fellow. He will whisper whatever is needed into your ear to misdirect you from your purpose, your potential, your mission—that thing you were created to do, and most importantly, from the authentic person you were created to be. Root will distract you from your *intended function*, your *teleios*. Whatever it is you are, Root will most assuredly tell you,

"You are not." Don't listen to him.

Some people don't even know Root's name or that he exists. Root is that voice in your head that immobilizes you. It brings fear where there is none, or exaggerates fear to confuse you or throw you off course. It is the lying voice of distraction. It is the voice that says you are someone other than who God created/intended you to be.

Using the Manual

You know how a new appliance or other household item comes with an instruction manual, telling you how to best use the product, what to do when something goes wrong, what numbers to call when you need help, plus other information to help you derive the best use out of the product? Well, God knows what he did when he created you. We must listen for His voice as we walk our daily life. He will instruct us in the way we should go, what we should do, and the best use of our time and resources in doing it. God wants us to cultivate the art of Being. When we listen to Satan, it's like taking the owner's manual and throwing it in the drawer (which is exactly what most of us do with the new appliance's manual), and then listening to our know-it-all neighbor who tells us to "stick a hanger in it to get good reception." We do that, instead of referring to the manual. In this case the "manual" is the Word of God or God's voice. Instead of referring to God's voice, we defer to that other voice in our head, the one that does not have our good in mind. The one whose purpose is to baffle and disrupt.

While God is a Gentleman, Satan has no nobility whatsoever. He did, once upon a time, but he abdicated it in pursuit of God's throne (Ezekiel 28:11-19). Ever since then, he's been after the heart of man, and in many cases, winning some of those hearts over. While God will never force you to do anything, Satan will try to force you through strong emotions such as guilt and shame. He will tell you that "you may as well…" or "if you don't…" which could coerce you to respond to his suggestion instead of taking the time to think and pray through your options.

While God can be persuasive but gentle at the same time, Satan will be malicious in his persuading. He is loud and again, demanding of an immediate response or quick decision. While God says, "this is what you ought to do"—even though you should be obedient to Him, he leaves it up to you—Satan screams, "this is what you *have* to do!" Thoughts from him are often sudden intrusions. So, when intense pressure comes with a thought, reject it immediately. This is an example of not being impulsive. Acting under compulsion is like a thought that comes into your mind, one that requires an action on your part with no space for consideration. You act and then regret. You regret and then look for someone to blame and the cycle continues.

Satan's voice gives a sense of despair that all is lost,

even if all isn't lost. If it's coming from him, it's a lie that is to be rejected. Again, he's always lied and is always lying. Thoughts originating from him often bring a sense of helplessness, when the truth is you have everything you need in Christ (2 Peter 1:3). You either have the resources with you, within your grasp, or they will be provided for you. You are not helpless. And you are not alone. Thoughts originating from Satan often bring a sense of hopelessness if you continue down the path.

As followers of Jesus, with the Holy Spirit, we have the God of hope (Romans 15:13) living in us, as part of our being. Satan will tell us all is lost when God says He will not allow us to be tempted beyond what you we bear, but when we are tempted, He will provide a way out of it (1 Corinthians 10:13). Some people misinterpret 1 Corinthians 10:13 to mean He won't give us more than we can handle, but that's not what He is saying. God will often give us more than we can handle, so that we turn to Him, and so that we can grow.

Isaiah 48:10-11 says, "See, I have refined you, though not as silver; I have tested you in the furnace of affliction. For my own sake, I do this. How can I let myself be defamed? I will not yield my glory to another" (NIV). Some people see God as egotistical because He desires glory for His name. I've wondered about this too, when someone sees fit to share their doubts with me and with others in hopes of changing a person's perspective of God. Let me put it to you this way. God IS. He is The

Great I AM. He made all things, and through Him all things have their life and their being (Acts 17:28). His refining you for His glory is not because He is narcissistic as some have accused Him of being.

In his book, *Waking the Dead*, John Eldridge stated, "The Glory of God is man fully alive." (2) When we live in our true self, if we live through our talents, if we reflect who we really are and were meant to be instead of being mired down in our mistakes or mistakes of others, when we are not stuck in regret and "if only's," we reflect the glory of God. Glorifying God actually benefits us! We operate from our original design.

Most of us operate out of fear or labels that others, and sometimes we ourselves, devise for us. We make a mistake, and we decide that we are a failure. Failing at something doesn't make us a failure. It may mean that we've failed at that particular thing, but it often means we need to try another direction.

When we believe God and that we are who He made us to be, we will be able to grasp this truth. He is the way, the truth, and the life (John 14:6). There are many things in life that are too difficult to handle without Him. People try. People fail. They put themselves through so much stuff that isn't necessary, and it's heartrending. The old hymn, "What a Friend We Have in Jesus," puts it succinctly, "Oh, what peace we often forfeit. Oh, what needless pains we bear, all because we do not carry everything to God in prayer."

Rejoice that He does give us more than we can

handle. He is cultivating us. Helping us to become the persons He originally created us to be. When we go through trials and we lean on God and on the community in which He has placed us, we are transformed. We change. We grow. We become close to who we were originally intended to be.

Satan isn't interested in any of this. He doesn't love you. He hates you because he hates God. He wants to use you to hurt yourself and to ultimately hurt God. He has no interest in your well-being.

Stop listening to him. Learn to turn off the voice whenever its frequency pushes its way into your mind. In the following chapter, we will take a look at the voice that over time has become even more distracting than Satan's.

Chapter Five

Competing Voice #3 – Society

Of the four voices, Society's voice, is the most complicated because it is multifaceted. Constant information streams in from a variety of different avenues: radio, television, magazines, newspapers, billboards, bus benches, the sides of buses, license plate frames, monitors atop gas pumps, t-shirts, the backs of receipts, the fences surrounding the baseball infield, the front edge of the scorekeepers table directly across from the camera at basketball games, and the sides of ink pens, and the hundreds of social media apps. All the messages are sometimes subtly but always brazenly coercing us into their belief systems and expectations: try this, buy that; adjust this, change that; start this, stop that; believe this, ignore that.

Here's the issue: God is saying one thing at any given

time, but Society's voice is saying many things all at once, and Society's voice speaks with authority. But it is not an authority unless you let it.

Anyone can open an online account, be it one of the social-media platforms, a YouTube channel, or purchase air-time on any local television or radio program. As soon as that account hit the airwaves, it becomes one of the facets of Society's voice. Just because someone is spouting information in an authoritative manner doesn't mean they are actually an authority on what they are talking about. And, people can be passionate and sincere, but also passionately and sincerely wrong at the same time. The trouble is the information is espoused as if it is the 'gospel' truth from people who have deemed themselves as authority figures. Are there authority figures on different topics? Of course, there are authorities, but in a culture where we have been bred to rely on the evening news where the information is just that—information about the goings-on of our communities and the world, we've learned over time to trust the screen and the people on it.

My undergraduate degree is in journalism. When I was in school, my professors told our cohort that as journalists, we would be the watchdogs of society. Our job was to tell the truth when government, corporations, or everyday people were doing things they were not supposed to do. We were tasked with keeping them honest by exposing them when they were not. Since my days in journalism school and my early years as a reporter, that accountability role seems to have slowly withered. Now anyone's agenda can be touted. On top of that, many of the media outlets are owned by the same corporations we would have been required to report on. If "they said it on the news," we've been conditioned to trust what is being fed to us.

In today's media, that same conditioning is going on, except that now the "reporters" are your average citizens handing out information to whoever will "like and subscribe" to their channel. Since we've been trained to rely on the screen and the professional journalists disseminating the information, relying on this new kind of reporter is nothing but a small leap to buying into whatever that new reporter writes or says. On top of that, so much information is coming in that we don't even really hear most of it anymore. The sound is static. Noise. White noise.

When scrolling through an app on the internet, most of us aren't even tuned in. We've learned to see but not see. When we peruse social media, many are doing the finger scroll, not even caring enough about what is being presented to stop and take a real look. If people are aiming for engagement through social media, they've learned to become more and more succinct about what they write or we'll just scroll past it like robots.

Much of what is posted isn't even read, at least not all the way through. I catch myself doing it. There's been times when I've been scrolling through, land on something interesting that may have ten pictures attached which might require a swipe to the left to see the post's entirety. I've never made it past three or four. When it's ten, there's no way.

The Society-voice can easily cause whiplash. On the one hand, the voice of Society promotes vanity and at times whispers, "It's all about you." On the other hand, it whispers, "You're not good enough. Nowhere near so-and-so," promoting insecurity.

Change the Channel

It's time to develop discernment. If we are to have any peace, we have to filter through the noise being fed to our minds and get rid of most of it. Paul talks about this in 2 Corinthians 10:5. He challenges us to stop the thoughts—the voices—from coming in. In today's language, I would imagine Paul urging people: "Stop the static." We have the power to do this, but we don't always use it. Many of us become prisoners of our thoughts, believing whatever comes into our minds, whether it is from the Self, Society, or Satan.

Having raised two teenaged girls, I have had a front row seat to the battle with the confusing voices that come out of nowhere and assault the mind. One of my daughters and I were riding along in the car, listening to music, and talking. Then there was a gap of silence. Nothing major, we'd just stopped talking for a bit and were enjoying the drive. I glanced over, and my daughter had tears on her cheeks.

"What's the matter? I asked.

"I'm crying because I'm sick of the large pores on my face."

Out of nowhere, she'd looked in the mirror of her visor to fix her hair, had a thought—"I have large pores"— believed it, had another thought—"this isn't fair,"—and began to cry.

Many of us spend much of our day like this. We're fine one minute, and the next, we're in a state of sadness.

You don't have to fall victim to this. Just as you can change the channel of a television, radio, or internet program, you can also change the channel of the voice you are listening to at any given moment. Tuning in and capturing the thoughts before they do damage takes skill and practice because for most people, it isn't something that comes naturally. But when you change the channel enough times, it can become as natural as breathing.

In that Corinthian passage, Paul talks about destroying arguments, lofty opinions, and pretensions that set themselves up against the knowledge of God. The IVP Background Bible Commentary says that Paul is actually using a war metaphor. He is saying we are doing battle with false ideas that push their way through to human thought. If the battle is for the mind's attention, then the battle has to be in the mind.

The Bible says we have the mind of Christ. This may be why Society feeds the human mind with a barrage of noise that leads to comparison, then insecurity, then self-doubt, and finally defeat and stagnation. After a while, people just get stuck, feel hopeless about change, and accept defeat. For Christians, that means accepting the loss as "just the way it is," and waiting for heaven.

A popular minister talks about living your best life in many of his books and in much of his preaching. Another preacher, Preacher B, not quite as popular, basically accused him of heresy, saying that it is impossible to live your best life here on earth because your best life isn't for here. Your best life won't happen until you get to heaven. Preacher B, like many Christians who have given up, espouses rhetoric that says, "Give up. Your best life is yet to come. You just have to wait to get to heaven to acquire it."

This is in direct opposition to Jesus. He said He came here so that we can have a full life (John 10:10). If Jesus meant "life to the full" to be something we enjoy on the other side, why doesn't He just take His people to Heaven as soon as they are saved? I believe He meant full life to be enjoyed now, although having life to the full in Heaven is a given.

Thought-Stopping

There are several ways to notice when your attention is arrested by Society's voice rather than that of the Savior's. As mentioned before, when listening to Society, you will find yourself comparing yourself to others, feeling insecure about who you are (and whose you are), doubting yourself, and then falling into defeat and stagnation. Below are tools for stopping these thought processes in their tracks when you find your attention captured by Society's channel.

1. Comparison:

While comparing and contrasting yourself with others is part of identity formation, that developmental window happens in the teen years with your peers. Unfortunately, with media in general and social media in particular, the necessary process that forms one's identity before adulthood is extending past teen and early adult years into parts of the life span it was never designed for. Teens use comparison to figure out where they stand when it comes to what they believe and prefer. Social comparison, in its healthy form can motivate a young person in this stage of development.

Comparison that doesn't motivate can become quite damaging to a person's sense of self and overall well-being. Comparison that leads to envy, self-disparagement, and regret isn't being used in a constructive and developmental manner. Scrolling through photos or images of carefully presented depictions of another person's life can leave adolescents believing they are not good enough, or they are not able to accomplish what they set out to do. Teens don't realize that what they are looking at has been carefully modified in order to garner a certain response. Sometimes the sought-after response is envy. At other times the teens curating the post is either consciously or unconsciously creating a narrative of their life that they want other people to believe. Unbeknownst to many, some people create this narrative hoping that they, themselves will one day believe it.

When comparison isn't creating motivation, it is likely creating anxiety because the teens look at another's success, good looks, and fun life, and think that their life doesn't measure up. In this case, comparison likely does the opposite and causes them to stop pursuing their goals altogether because they feel so inadequate.

One of the ways to decrease comparison on social media is to realize what you are seeing is not reality. Social media allows people to present a filtered sense of reality by presenting highlights rather than day-to-day realities of their lives. We stumble across these posts and think, "Why doesn't my life look like that?" Well, guess what? That person's life probably doesn't look like that either. Believe that and remind yourself that you are looking at someone's highlight reel and doctored-to-the-nines photos of themselves. You aren't really seeing the warts of a real life. It's not that you would wish anyone harm or wish that someone's life wasn't as fabulous as they are presenting. But with the right perspective, it's possible for you to take in the information with an acute sense that all that glitters isn't gold.

2. Insecurity:

Comparison often leads to insecurity. Society has a reason for making you compare yourself to others. It wants you to feel insecure so you can look to it for improvement. It's often about the dollar. Much of what you see in media in the form of commercials or ads is designed to convince you that you are lacking something they can easily provide. Be slimmer, smarter, prettier, and healthier when you buy this or that product.

Insecurity makes you very self-focused. Even when you make an improvement, there's always more you should do, according to the ads. You are the only person who can be you. There's no one else who can fit the bill, and there's no sense in trying to make yourself into someone else's image.

One of the ways to fend off insecurity is to know *whose* you are. Find out the truth of who you were created to be. Know your strengths and skill set and improve them to your liking, or for the purpose of contributing to society. This person or that person may be better than you at something, but so what? Whatever you have to bring to the table, bring it with all *you* are and all you've got. When you do this, you promote a sense of satisfaction on the inside. And you are more likely to celebrate someone's success when you are feeling good about your own sense of self or set of accomplishments.

3. Self-Doubt:

Self-doubt, like any of the other side effects of Society's voice, can lead to depression, anxiety, and most of all, procrastination, or a lack of motivation. Self-doubt stops you from engaging in the one-foot-in-front-of-the-other behavior that allows you to complete goals. A cycle begins because when you don't do the work, you won't complete the goal, and when you don't complete the goal, you end up affirming to yourself that you "can't do it" or you "aren't good enough to do it." Therefore, overcoming the self-doubt cycle takes intention.

If you are trying to accomplish anything at all, it's a form of self-care to break the self-doubt cycle with intention and diligence. If you decide to tackle self-doubt, especially for the purpose of turning down the voices that compete with the Savior's voice, here are some tools to apply at any time and any place:

a. Recall and write down past accomplishments. Recollection reminds you that you can in fact complete what you set out to do.

b. Become mindful of the thoughts passing in and out of your consciousness. This is really the crux of this book. In order to banish negative thoughts, you must first be aware of them in order to stop them by applying some of what you are learning here. Most of the negative thoughts that enter your consciousness come in through the back door of the subconscious or unconscious parts of the mind. You don't consciously notice them, but you just start feeling bad as a result of their presence. You might feel sadness or despair, anxiety, or a sense of being stuck. Bringing into your awareness thoughts that are scrolling through allows you to challenge the thoughts with truth or replace them with another equally true version of what is real.

c. Identify what matters most to you. The list of these most important things makes up your Value System. Your values govern your behavior, whether or not you are aware of what they are. Becoming aware of your values can be beneficial in helping you see the fruitlessness of much of what Society's voice offers. If what you are enticed to compare doesn't even matter to you, why spend any time or mental energy on it? For example, if Society has decided you should be offended by something that isn't aligned with your value system, you may have subconsciously agreed. You get offended by something someone says, and you don't even know why. If you were truly upset, you would either know right away or after a time of reflection. If nothing comes after some internal investigation, you are probably borrowing offense based on someone else's agenda. Release it. You have your own mind. Don't abdicate your emotional energy to someone else's indignation.

d.   There are other ways to seek help, but they can't necessarily be applied any time and any place. If you are encountering an especially difficult stretch, it may be helpful to spend time with people who are supportive and affirming. Sometimes you have to spend time with people who believe in you in order for that belief to rub off. Another way is to seek professional help. Not all clients who call me for therapy are calling me for help with depression, anxiety, or relationship difficulties. Some are calling due to issues going on with their self-esteem or because they are having difficulty moving forward in their lives.

4.   **Defeat:**

A defeat mindset says, "Why bother?" Once trapped in this mindset, a person can be imprisoned for years or even her whole life. Ever wonder why some people never seem to catch a break? Sometimes part of this is because she has adopted the "why bother" mindset. She believes nothing ever goes right for her so there isn't any point in trying. She's given up and has resorted to robotically passing through life in a rote manner without much hope of anything ever improving or changing. She's convinced her existence will not make much of an impact on the planet or eternity. The defeated mindset is one that stays where it is for fear of disappointment. The defeated mindset is a place where dreams die and goals are no longer thought of, much less set. A mind shift is

needed to overcome a defeated mindset. How do you know you have landed in a defeated mindset?
    a.   You believe things will never work out for you.
    b.   You believe it's too late for you.
    c.   You believe you should have gone for your dreams earlier in life and now you are too old, or there are so many young people doing what you should have been doing years ago, it would take forever to catch up. The problem with this way of thinking is the fact that there is no need to catch up. What you have to offer from your point of view, no one else can offer or supply, even if what others are offering is similar. In order to overcome a defeated mindset, you must exchange it for a triumphant mindset. A triumphant mindset helps you understand that where you have been often has nothing to do with where you are going. You can, however, use the experiences of where you have been to rule out barriers to where you want to reach. Thomas Edison *failed* at creating the light bulb thousands of times. He didn't see these attempts as failures. He saw them as ways not to make a light bulb and kept going until he had success.

    To develop a triumphant mindset, use the following:
    i.   Acknowledge that you are doing something new or hard but also important. If it weren't important, even if only to you, you would not have established it as a goal. Once you've acknowledged whatever is needed, you push through and begin with your new starting point. Make a to-do list. What is the first thing to do? Start there and then move on to the next thing on the list. Once you're involved and, on the move, your mind will switch

from "I can't" to "I'm doing" because you are in fact engaged in doing something.

ii. Imagine what your life will look like when you are successful in doing what you want. If you're trying to overcome procrastination, imagine yourself giving time to your project or whatever it is you want to engage in each day. See yourself getting up early or staying up a little later to give a half hour to the project you'd wish to complete. What would that feel like? I do this whenever I fall off of my running or exercise routine. I imagine what it feels like to get in an early morning run and how it positively impacts the rest of my day and my sleep later that evening. Since I've been through this several times, I'm aware of the sense of accomplishment I feel, and I'm encouraged to get back out there.

iii. Learn and utilize the Kaizen Method: a mindset or way of behaving that sees progress as attainable in small, constant, positive improvements. The Kaizen principles are sort of the "how to climb a mountain" approach—one step at a time. In this method you can take note of and relish your small wins along the way instead of worrying about the monumental project ahead of you. A defeatist mindset most assuredly can be overcome and it must be overcome to avoid that part of the Society voice that ultimately tries to encourage you to stop.

5. Stagnation:

Stagnation is a cessation of movement, a lack of growth. I once read a novel about a man who'd accidently ended up in hell. While running from some thugs, he ran into an abandoned building and accidentally stumbled upon some portal to hell. The story was like a modern-day take on *Dante's Inferno*. The nine levels of hell represented what hell would look like today.

The premise of the book is that hell changes and worsens over the centuries due to the sins in which man gets involved here on earth. In this version of the nine circles of hell, one of the levels is represented by people sitting in easy chairs in front of television screens. Their eyes are just staring as into a void, into the static screen of the television while their hands and feet are stuck in buckets of maggots and slime. Their eternity ends up being a version of how they lived their lives—pursuing nothing, going nowhere, glued in front of a screen that had nothing to offer their progress in life. With nothing to help them grow, they became stagnant in life after they gave up and gave in to the noise of static all around them. Years of stagnation took away their opportunities for growth and development.

Can social media be used for growth and development? It absolutely can! There are people out there helping others, providing information for growth, for a better life, a fuller existence. The problem is, there is so much information, so much noise, that if not properly self-regulated, the user of social media can end up being pulled into static.

One of the definitions of static is "acting as weight but not moving." Much of what you hear from Society's voice is this kind of static. The information (static) coming from the voice sounds important, leaving the notion that what you are hearing is needed or helpful, but in the end, what's being said doesn't move you to do anything. Part of that could just be your problem because when you learn something and you don't apply it, the benefit of what you learned is lost because it isn't integrated into your way of being. But I believe part of the static is a natural outcome. There is so much to choose from, it becomes paralyzing. This is called *option paralysis*. Another part of the problem with static just may be because much of what is being touted out in the media really isn't saying much of anything.

Recognizing the patterns that ultimately lead to your doing nothing with your life is of utmost importance. What ultimately leads to your not putting forth the effort to create the life you want? What stops you from following your dreams or accomplishing your goals? Use what you read here to recognize whether you've entered into the pattern of comparison, insecurity, self-doubt, defeat, and stagnation. Turn away from these patterns or tendencies before you are drawn into the nothingness where the voice of Society wishes to leave you.

Society's Influence on Your Thinking

Patterns always lead somewhere. God says one thing is not okay, and Society says it is okay over and over, until at last we believe that what God says is not true or no longer pertains to today's society. It is imperative to guard your heart and mind against the different channels of Society. Be mindful of what voice is feeding your soul. Everything God serves is true soul food, so make the quality choice to listen to the Savior and ignore the voice of Society.

Society informs your thinking through media, academia, community, cultural norms, family, and churches. Not all of the input is bad or necessarily opposed to God's influence on our thought life. But if we want to minimize the interference of what God has to say in our lives, it behooves us to be aware of what Society is declaring and how it jives with what God declares.

It is important for us to be aware of the thoughts that pass through our minds because what happens there directly impacts our behaviors and our attitudes. What information are we taking in? Is it information we believe without question? Are we aware enough of our own minds to realize we are forming opinions especially when receiving new information that was not previously our own?

First Corinthians says that we believers have the mind of Christ (vs. 2:16). Second Peter 1:3-4 tells us that God has set us up to be able to have what we need to live a godly life through our knowledge of Him. So, we have to gain knowledge of God. How do we do that? Through His Word and through spiritual practices. God wants us to learn, think through, and pass on our knowledge of Him and what He has set up in the world. The deception that comes from Society seeks to occupy our time, all mixed up by the aforementioned patterns in order to divide the human race.

We are polarized as a nation. Just take a look at news reels from the Covid year, 2020. In addition to a pandemic, North Americans struggled with racial and civil unrest. People from both sides participating in those rallies spouted beliefs that were supported by their choice of news media.

A documentary called *The Social Dilemma* (1) discussed how social-media platforms are designed to keep our eyes on the screen. The platforms have become savvy at predicting our behavior and at delivering to us what our itching ears want to hear. When you do a search, you get results that are consistent with what you already believe. Your newsfeeds contain advertisements filled with products based on what you've searched for in the past, so you are more likely to buy them. Notifications are set up to get your eyes back onto the screen.

It's true. I have two Instagram accounts: One for my therapy practice: @healingthemindandspirit, and one for my writing: @tracytaris. When I first started the latter, I wasn't consistent in posting on it. One day I posted something, and two days later, my @healingthemindandspirit account received a notification that @tracytaris "just posted in a while." This wasn't true. It was as if the notification's goal was to get me to reach for my phone to see what @tracytaris had "just posted," when it was actually posted a few days earlier. Social media and the hands behind it use ultra-savvy tactics to capture our attention.

Social media is great with *confirmation bias*, which is the idea that you only tune in to things that reinforce what you already believe. Social unrest received a lot of help because of confirmation bias, in that a person's beliefs are constantly reinforced by information coming across their screens as a result of their searches.

It is almost impossible to receive a different opinion because what you think is reinforced over and over. That's why you'll hear people say things like, "How can they believe thus and so; don't they see this?" The answer is, "No, they don't." They aren't taking in the same information that you are because their search results align with what they already believe, just as your search results align with what you already believe. So, the old adage "taking something with a grain of salt," should be applied toward incoming information.

Society's voice has many voices within itself and many goals: distraction, diversion for the purpose of polarization or selling, and most of all, inundation with information that leaves us paralyzed in our growth process. It's time to learn to tune into the one true voice—the only One that matters. The voice that loves us with a deep love many of us have taken for granted our whole life.

Chapter Six
Competing Voice #4 – The Savior

Romans 8:16 says, "The Spirit Himself bears witness with our spirit that we are children of God" (ASV). God speaks to your spirit because that is where He lives—within you. First Corinthians 6:17 says those who are united with the Lord are united with Him in spirit.

God is a gentleman. He will never speak in a forceful or demanding way. He is gentle, firm in His conviction, and persuasive to the open heart. God is omnipotent. He can override your free will if He wants to—He's just that powerful, but He will never allow his persuasion to override your free will. Because of His great love and because He wants our love to be freely given, He chooses not to override man's free will. That's good news because it also means He won't allow anyone else to override your free will either.

Although Satan was expelled from heaven to Earth (Ezekiel 28:17), and he has some free reign here (1 John

5:19, 1 Peter 5:8), He will never be allowed to override your free will. The saying, "The devil made me do it," is false. The devil can't make any of us do anything. We've discussed some of the attributes of God's voice in the previous chapter. In this one, you'll learn how to tell the difference between Satan's voice and God's.

God will tell you what you "ought" to do because what you ought to do is good, and it is right for you and others around you. But He leaves the actual decision up to you. He won't harass you into the outcome you ought to take. And trust me, if it is coming from God, you definitely *ought* to do it. I'm just saying. People may harass you at times, and I'd bet Satan is harassing you too, but God won't do it. He may put people in your life to help you see the wisdom in the correct decision, but He always leaves the final choice up to you. That is free will.

When God speaks, His voice gives you a sense of peace, and a sense that everything will be okay. Even if you can't see how everything will be okay, and even if what He says feels a bit scary to you, God's voice still leaves you with a sense of peace. His speaking to you and guiding you comes from His peace.

The rub comes in when dealing with the sense that everything is going to be okay. We may derive a sense of peace (and if the voice is coming from God, there *is* peace), but you may not have trained yourself in the art and discipline of listening to God in order to align your feelings with your belief.

I've spoken with people who have felt a sense that everything was going to be okay when things were seemingly falling apart. They couldn't see how things were going to work out, but they had a gut feeling that they would. These people go with this feeling and choose to trust. Then there are others who have a gut feeling that things are going to be okay, but get caught in the snare of not being able to work out in their minds *how* it will be okay. They give way to fear. Anxiety about not seeing how it'll all work out sets in. It is scary to them to have to wait on the outcome, so they choose to give in to fear instead of resting in the peace that could be theirs.

Directives from God are clear and distinctive, but life circumstances and sometimes certain personality traits can hinder one's ability to hear from God. With practice in tuning in, barriers to hearing God can be overcome. Aspects of our own psyche—grief, unprocessed issues, woundedness, a lack of time in prayer and in the Word—can muffle our ability to hear God, but He speaks anyway. His voice is sure for God is sure.

God doesn't desire to confuse you. Confusion means lack of understanding, uncertainty, a disorderly jumble, the state of being bewildered or unclear in one's mind about something. If you feel any of these things, the voice is definitely not God's voice. It is the voice of Satan, or it is the voice of your own anxiety. If you are lacking clear direction, go to the Lord and wait. "I wait for the Lord, my soul doth wait, and in His Word, do I put my hope" (Psalm 130:5 [KJV]). The Message version translates this verse like this, "I pray to God—my life a prayer—and wait for what He'll say and do it." Wait. God is okay with us waiting and taking the time to learn to discern His will. How do we wait? Here are five suggestions to help you in the waiting:

1.Pray.

Prayer itself can be an act of waiting. Later you will learn about different forms of prayer, but the act of waiting can be prayer itself. Waiting can be a posture of humble anticipation in which you expect an answer but train yourself to relax into God's timing. Waiting can also be a time when you talk with Him each day as a check-in. "Where are we with this, God?" I'm laughing at myself as I'm writing this because I'm sure I've asked this of Him before.

2.Switch your focus.

Once you have made your request, give thanks and praise to God for what He has already done in your life, especially if it pertains in any way to what you are currently waiting for. For instance, if you are praying about whether you should change employment, give thanks that you have a job in the first place. Americans are always accused of having *first-world problems*, meaning some of the worries we have are concerns that are lower on the worry chain, (or not even on the worry chain) for people in third-world countries. For example, some people may stress over which restaurant to go out to; whereas, others are worried about how they are going to put food on their table. Switch your focus to what you already have, and give praise to God as you wait for His response.

3. Prepare.

Let's say you are waiting for a response about switching jobs. In the meantime, make sure you are above board at your current place of employment. Don't act like one who is on her way out because you may not be. Acting like that is a dishonorable way to behave at your place of employment. Instead, do some research on the type of job or company you are considering. Beef up your resume and craft a well-worded cover letter for the type of position you are pursuing. You do your best for your part and let God lead you to His best.

4. Get a new perspective.

Every day of our lives should be lived as "God's will be done." Many times, we want what we want, but what we want may not be the best for us. This truth reminds me of a parable I once read about trusting God.

A man lived in a country that bordered a country with which the threat of war was a constant fear. The man, a farmer, had a prized horse he loved. The horse jumped over the fence of its pen, crossed that boundary line, and went into the hostile country.

The man's neighbors exclaimed, "Oh, that's too bad."

The man replied, "Maybe it's good."

A few weeks later, the horse returned leading a beautiful white stallion back to the pen.

The neighbors said, "Oh, that's good."

The man said, "Maybe it's bad."

The man's son took the stallion to try to break him, but he fell off the wild horse and broke his leg.

The neighbors pitied the man and said. "Oh, that's bad."

The man said, "Maybe it's good."

A week later, the countries went to war with each other. All of the young men in the man's country were drafted to fight in the war and they all died, except for the man's son, who couldn't be drafted due to his broken leg. (1)

The moral of the story? We like to label things as good or bad when it doesn't matter. According to Romans 8:28, God works for His people's good. What seems like a good thing can actually lead to something bad, and what seems like a bad thing can actually lead to something good. Whatever the circumstance, God works. We can choose to submit to His plan or push through with our own. His plan, even when we can't see the why or how of it, is infinitely better than what we can create for ourselves.

5. Live your life.
What are the things that need tending to? Tend to them. While you are waiting, don't behave as if you are in limbo. What in your life requires action on your part? Tomorrow has enough trouble of its own, so don't borrow from it today.

Speak, for Your Servant is Listening

God speaks to us all the time; we just aren't listening all the time. Most assuredly, when we need Him and we call out, He speaks. He will answer an invitation we extend when we are seeking Him or listening for Him. He says so, "Then you will call on me and come and pray to me, and I will listen to you. You will seek me and find me when you seek me with all your heart" (Jeremiah 29:12-13 [NIV]).

How God speaks to us depends largely on our personality, how we are made, and on our particular relationship with Him. Because God meets us where we are, He will not speak to us in a way we do not understand. Our level of understanding doesn't matter to Him. He wants to meet with us through prayer and through the influence of the Holy Spirit.

Romans 14 discusses people's different levels of faith—what some believe, what makes others stumble, and how God accepts people where they are. In the same way, God will find a way to speak with you in a manner in which you will understand. Think of the relationships you have. Whether you're addressing your children, siblings, parents, or friends, how you speak to them differs because they are each different. You know how to present a particular kind of information to each of them because of your understanding of who they are.

God does the same thing. Don't be intimidated by someone else's reported experience of hearing from God or of their relationship with God. Pray and ask for discernment of how He speaks to and shows up for *you*. Once you've tapped into your unique relationship with God, you'll find it easier to hear from Him. Some people have termed this concept *Spiritual Temperament*. Just as we have a *Personality Temperament*, we have a spiritual temperament. Your spiritual temperament points to the kind of ways you are likely to hear from or experience God.

A good reference book for this is Gary Thomas' *Sacred Pathways*. (2) In it, he talks about nine different spiritual temperaments that speak to the different ways people tend to experience and pray to God. Thomas encourages people to explore their spiritual temperaments by doing a little self-examining to discern what theirs might be. Thomas encourages the reader to think through the different people and stories in the Bible. He leads the reader to decide with whom they relate, pay attention to what makes their heart sing, and tune into what makes them think about or want to praise God.

For example, *Sacred Pathways* suggests if you like to take hikes. and while out there you feel attached to the glory and beauty of nature, you may be a *naturalist*. People who are naturalists feel closer to God outdoors. They are the people who like to take prayer walks more than they like to be on their knees. These people may not even like being on their knees! They are no less "spiritual" than the person on her knees. They are just different.

Another example are the people who like to read through and pray through prayers in the Bible or prayers written by others. These people are the *traditionalists*.

They enjoy ritual and sacrament. Growing up Catholic, this is primarily the way I was trained in prayer. Though I am no longer a practicing Catholic, I still very much enjoy ritual in my prayer life. I love lighting candles. I don't simply use The Lord's Prayer as a blueprint; I find comfort in actually praying it and reflecting on the different components of it.

This brings me to another spiritual temperament, the *contemplative*. Contemplatives love to do just what the name suggests, contemplate. Their prayer life is filled with thinking on the meaning of what God is teaching them. Prayer for them may take the form of one of the prayers I will discuss later, *Lectio Divina*, which is a divine reading of the scripture. Contemplatives will read a passage or pray a prayer and then think about the various meanings of the passage or wonder why they uttered a prayer that sprang from their hearts.

None of these people are wrong simply because God isn't wrong. He knew what he was doing when He created them, and He loves what He created. Other temperaments Thomas discusses in *Sacred Pathways* are the *sensates* who love God through the arts, the *ascetics* who love God in silence and simplicity, and the *activists,* who love God through social confrontation. The *caregivers* love God through acts of service, *enthusiasts* love God primarily through worship, and *intellectuals* love God through study of the Word or certain doctrines. The intellectual has to understand faith. That may sound like an oxymoron, but it isn't. God is okay with us thinking about why we believe.

I highly recommend *Sacred Pathways* as it is one of the most respectful Christian books I have ever read. Many of us grew up in churches where we were taught to have morning prayer on our knees and bible study daily. While there is nothing wrong with that, God is a God of variety. Look around. Is there only one brand of flower or one brand of lily or rose for that matter? Explore! Your exploration may open up your receiver to hear God's broadcasting voice in ways you've never imagined.

God Versus Self

Because some people have heavy experiences with guilt and shame, they often confuse God's voice with the Self Voice. While God's voice will often convict us with specifics, He won't shame us. Our feelings of shame may be a product of our own filters, experiences, or beliefs about ourselves. Satan's voice tries to throw you off course or keep you stuck in some way.

Guilt, on the other hand, comes from the inside. It's actually a gift from God that alerts us when we are doing something we need to stop or when we have done something for which we need to apologize. Guilt is more about information we use to go down a different path. It isn't about us as people; it's more about a behavior that needs to be addressed. It's a fail-safe that without it, we wouldn't be considered normal.

In the psychology profession, there is a personality disorder whereby the guilt chip isn't present inside the person. They don't feel remorse for the wrong they do, and some of them even feel glee for the wrong they do. We live in a culture now that advocates for the silence of guilt. "You shouldn't feel guilty," it says. Well, yes, you should if there is something you have done wrong. To silence guilt completely runs the risk of our society becoming heartless and ruthless. When we feel guilty, we ought to ask ourselves, "Have I done something wrong?" If we are, fix it. We may very well be hearing from the Savior voice trying to help us correct our course.

When God speaks, He doesn't speak in generalities. We will clearly have no doubt about what needs to be repented of and what needs to be confessed. When God is specific, we'll get a sense like, "You were harsh with your co-worker today. You need to apologize." We'll feel a conviction about the situation in our spirit. We may resist with some sort of "but"; however, the path to obedience to hear God's voice is to submit in obedience when this occurs. In this specific example, this is what should happen:

1. Confess in prayer to God, and if needed, confess to a brother or sister in Christ,
2. Ask the Holy Spirit to give you a heart of repentance plus courage and conviction to follow through,

3. Go apologize to your co-worker, and
4. Ask if there is anything you can do to make amends.

Listening for God's voice is an old tradition that dates back to the mystics. Many of today's Christians do not follow this tradition. We should. As in anything, practice increases your ability to hear. Patience increases your desire to want to listen. Why? Because you will be richly rewarded with the assurance that the presence of God brings. It's all about discernment. Pray and ask the Holy Spirit to increase your ability to discern God's voice from that of Satan, Self, and Society. The more filled you are with the Spirit, the less you tune into the other distracting voices.

Voices that aren't God's will become dim until they fade completely into the background. When a person receives the gift of the Holy Spirit, He goes into your spirit. We are three-part beings, just as God is. He is Father, Son, and Holy Spirit. We are spirit, soul, (which houses the mind and emotions), and body.

Some people think soul and spirit are synonymous with each other, that they are two ways of discussing the same part of the person. But the Holy Scriptures differentiates between soul and spirit and states that the two can be separated. "For the Word of God is quick, and powerful, and sharper than any two-edged sword, piercing even to the dividing asunder of soul and spirit, and of joints and marrow, and is a discerner of the thoughts and intents of the heart" (Hebrews 4:12 [KJV]).

Just as it is an obvious, visible fact that the joints are a different part of the body than is the marrow, it is also an obvious invisible fact (according to God's Word), that the soul is a different part of the person than the person's spirit. To further help with this understanding on a human level, what do you think psychology is the study of? If you google it, you may get an answer something like, "Psychology is the study of the mind, emotions, and human behavior." And it is that, too, but the original Greek definition lists psychology as the study of the soul.

Using God's Word to Hear Him

When listening for God's voice, it is also important to note that His voice will always give you the truth and will respect your boundaries as to whether or not you follow that truth. Many of us want to follow, but hindrances prevent us from doing so. This is no excuse. I've heard people excusing themselves when doing something that wasn't good, by stating "God knows my heart." That statement is supposed to be enough to excuse them of doing wrong or hurting someone. Sure, God knows if you desire to do the right thing, but what you will be judged on is whether or not you follow through on the desire to do right. Second Corinthians 5:10 tells us that Christ will judge each of us for the things we do while here on Earth.

We all have choice. We are not judged on what we intend to do here in this life, but on what we actually do.

Romans 2:5-6 says our stubbornness and unrepentance will only bring God's wrath when He comes in judgment. We will either see eternal life with Him for the good we choose. Or, those of us who reject His truth and follow evil, will experience His wrath.

We are not judged on what we meant to or didn't mean to say, but on what we actually said. Matthew 12:36 makes this clear. "And I say unto you, that every idle word that men shall speak, they shall give account thereof in the day of judgment" (ASV). So, it doesn't matter what you meant or that you "only said that because..." What matters is that it was said carelessly or without consideration of how it would impact the person hearing it. Don't rely on the adage, "God knows my heart." Yes, He does. And "out of the abundance of the heart, his (man's) mouth speaketh" (Luke 6:45b [ASV]). I would also venture to say that a person behaves out of the overflow of their heart as well.

God speaks through His Word. Familiarize yourself with it by reading it, listening to it, studying it, journaling or writing about it, asking questions about it of people who may be wiser in the faith, and asking questions of God about it in prayer. Research what certain passages mean and what words in the context of a particular passage mean. You can even go deeper into study of God's word by doing hermeneutical evaluations (interpretation of language) and exegesis (discovering what words or concepts meant to people at the time).

You can familiarize yourself with memorizing the

Word and with practicing or living it. One of my colleagues, a therapist and minister, uses an acrostic for learning how to live the Word. When you R.E.A.D the Bible, take it a step further and initiate application by journaling what you read.

R. – Reflect. Think on what you just read. Ask God what He wants you to learn from the passage. What do you need to take away from it with whatever you are going through? Write down whatever comes to you. Then think on it—meditate—to see what ideas come to you. The Bible tells us to savor its words.

E. – Envision. Imagine what the passage looks like in practice in your day-to-day life. Think about people through whom you've seen this passage come to life and imagine ways to imitate them. Envision the fruit of practicing or living this scripture. Will it bring you more love, joy, peace, forbearance, kindness, goodness, faithfulness, gentleness, and self-control? Will it bring those fruit of the Spirit to others, through you? With diligence and practice, it will! Can you envision it? Can you imagine it? That's because the Word of God was written by the Holy Spirit. These are the fruit of Him, Holy Spirit. How could living these words not bring about this promise of Galatians 5:22? How could putting them into practice not cultivate you into the person God originally intended you to be? After all, God created the world with His Word and He created you by his Word; He spoke you into existence. By His Word you have life. You are sustained. He is the bread of life.

After His baptism, Jesus went into the wilderness to be tempted by Satan. After His 40-day fast, Satan came and tested Him saying, "If you are the Son of God, tell these stones to become bread."

Jesus answered, "It is written: 'Man shall not live on bread alone, but on every word that comes from the mouth of God.'"

Jesus was hungry, but His answer wasn't just to Satan. It was to us who would come to believe. And He isn't just talking about food you consume. He is talking about anything that we turn to for sustenance when our spiritual sustenance should come from the One true and living God—Father, Son and Holy Spirit. If you came from God—and, dear heart, you did—then operating as He created you connects you to the source of all life: Him, The Great I Am. Envision not settling for less. Imagine being who you are meant to be if you only believe what God's Word says in your everyday walking, talking, living, breathing life!

A. - Act or Action. What action can you take today to live out or practice what you have just read about? Let's take a look at an example of what I call a *directive scripture*. A directive scripture, from a definition I came up with to help me live out the scriptures, is one in which God gives us a direction—something to do.

In Matthew 28:19, Jesus tells the disciples to go and make disciples of the whole world. The "do" in this Scripture is to "go" and "make." If you are reading this passage and applying the R.E.A.D acrostic, the action you'd do would be to engage in behaviors that very day that carry out this command, or connect with someone to help her become a disciple of Jesus. That may involve studying the Bible with her, but it also may involve planting a seed by following a prompting in your heart to share your conversion story or to share a story of yours about when God worked in your life.

People are inspired by stories. I believe that is the reason Jesus taught in parables. It is the reason the movie industry has been one of the most popular forms of entertainment since its inception. Moviegoers identify with the characters and situations in a story. They see themselves, and that is where the connection lies. When you are applying the act part of this acrostic, try to think of something you can do to carry out what you just learned. It may be as simple as giving a prayer of thanks to God. It may be the act of writing down your thoughts in a journal. At any rate, the more interaction you have with scripture, the more likely it is to become more a part of the fiber of your being.

D. – Determine. Here you would determine to do the action written in your R.E.A.D. acrostic. An action that is written down is nothing but an intention until you actually carry it out. In Luke 9:44, Jesus started to tell His disciples what would happen to Him soon. He told them He'd be handed over for crucifixion, "delivered into the hands of men" (KJV). For some reason, the Holy Spirit prevented the disciples from discerning what He meant. The Bible says the meaning was hidden from them so they didn't understand what He was talking about. Verse 45 concludes by highlighting that the disciples were afraid to even ask Jesus about it.

Whether out of fear for what Jesus would say, or embarrassment that they'd been with Him all this time and still didn't know what He was talking about half the time, they chose the good old-fashion human route of not dealing with the uncertainty. Instead, they tried to distract themselves and probably Him too. First, they launched into an argument about who would be the greatest among them. The ever-patient Jesus used this distraction as a teaching opportunity to tell them the importance of childlikeness and probably the value of listening.

The next distraction was a subject change, one designed to make themselves look good to the Master. "Oh, and somebody had the nerve to drive out demons in your name but we tried to stop him because he is not one of us" (my paraphrase). Again, Jesus in His patience, used the distraction as a teaching opportunity letting them know that whoever is not against Him is for Him in the battle of soul winning.

After this second deflection, the Word states, He "resolutely set out for Jerusalem." I picture this scene as Jesus thinking something like, *Man, I just can't get through to these knuckleheads, so let me just do what my Father intends me to do next.*

Listen and Deal with It

Jesus tried to warn them at the beginning of verse 44 in Luke chapter 9 when He told them what was going to happen to Him. In giving the disciples credit, as a therapist, I imagine that on some level they knew what He was talking about. Matthew records three instances where He'd spoken of it before: Matthew 16:21-23, Matthew 17:22-23, and Matthew 20:17-19. Their deflections could have been their way of avoiding a stressful conversation. Kind of like when people can't handle the truth for fear of the action they would have to take afterwards, or for fear of the pain they'd feel when in-the-know. Maybe the disciples just didn't want to deal with the truth they were hearing. In psychology we call this *denial*. Denial is often seen as a bad state of being, and in some instances, it can be. But in other instances, it's just a form of survival, a way for a person to cope until she has the tools to handle the crisis.

Jesus going to the cross would have been a crisis for His disciples for sure. At any rate, Jesus saw that He wasn't going to get through to them, at least not now, so He resolutely went on to Jerusalem to do what He'd come to the earth to do. *Resolute* means resolve. Another word for resolve is *determine*. To determine is to firmly decide to do something. That's the stance you have to train yourself to take in the determine part of the R.E.A.D acrostic. *If* you decide to use this acrostic to get to know God's Word and to hear His Voice. Again, an action is nothing more than an intention until it is acted upon. In your journal writing of R.E.A.D., determine that you will do whatever is necessary to carry out the action you wrote down in the A (action) part of the acrostic.

Part Two:
Static Interference:

Chapter Seven
Hindrance #1 – Relational Sin

While there are many hindrances that can get in the way of our ability to hear from the Lord, we will take a look at four of them: Relational Sin, Shame, Distraction, and Fear. Don't say: "Oh no, not another book about sin." Rest assured, the purpose of this section is not to wag my finger at shortcomings in our life. That's not my place. My place is in helping us see how people often do things they do not feel proud of and then condemn themselves to the point of incapacitating themselves from hearing God's voice.

One of the biggest areas in which we condemn ourselves is in our close relationships. Below is a tool that will be helpful in teaching us how to navigate a relationship after we've sinned against another person.

My great grandmother, Mama Lee, used to admonish people to "do right" by others. When she knew of discord within the relationship of two or more family members, and they somehow dragged her into it looking for pity, she'd simply tell them to "do right." The wisdom in this for the purpose of our study is rooted in 1 John 4:20

which says if you can't love your brother, then how can you love God? Love in the context of this Scripture isn't talking about a feeling. It is talking about love as an action. When we have done something to offend someone we love, we should follow Mama Lee's "do right" admonition and take responsibility for it.

In regard to our relationship with God, sin is not the problem. Jesus already took care of that. *Sin-consciousness* is the problem. For some people, all they think about is their sin and the sins of others. There are whole church congregations in which one of the main missions is sin-management. This comes in the form of controlling people, putting burdens and yokes on their shoulders, and then shaming and condemning them when they cannot carry those yokes and burdens.

Many Christians say they are grateful for what Christ did on the cross, but then they live their life trying to make up for sins of the past. They try to prove their worthiness of the gift of salvation or try to earn the salvation Christ already gave. God isn't concerned with sin the way they may think because He already made a way for the forgiveness of it. Does this mean we can just sin and not worry about it because the debt is already paid? No. Hebrews 10:26-31 says that if we keep on sinning, there is no sacrifice left for us because Jesus already paid the price for our sins. A close study of the Scripture will reveal a few meanings. Among them, Jesus already defeated sin and death on the cross. One of the reasons He did this is because sin separates us from

God. Jesus stood in the way of that separation and cleared the way for us to approach the throne with boldness (Hebrews 4:16).

When we do sin, what is needed is two things: confession and repentance. Confession is when we tell God or someone else about our sin for the purpose of clearing our conscience and processing sorrow. Repentance is when we choose to turn away from that sin and do it no more. Repentance is also changing your mind about something. In a way, choosing to tune into the Savior's voice more than the others mentioned is a form of repentance.

We confess to God for forgiveness of that sin (1 John 1:9) and we confess to each other for healing (James 5:16). Hebrews tells us that Jesus' blood has cleansed our consciences. The Bible says there is no condemnation for people of God (Romans 8:1), but people tend to disagree with the Bible in this regard and spend a lot of time condemning not only themselves but other people.

This perpetual condemnation is where boundaries come in. If you suffer from this, you have to decide within yourself whether you are going to buy into someone else's condemnation of you. A simple exercise in processing through this is asking yourself, "What is God's take on my sin?" One way to get His take is to ask, "Have I confessed it? Have I repented of it?" If the answer is yes to those, then it's a done deal. It doesn't matter if someone else lets you off the hook. It's not their hook to let you off of. Sin is between God and the sinner, not the sinner's fellow believer. When you sin against a person, you are to go to that person, confess and ask forgiveness, as per Matthew 18, then you let it go.

Confessing a sin and asking forgiveness are not so simple processes because of the vanishing conscience we are experiencing in our culture. By vanishing conscience, I mean the continuous act of silencing the conscience. With practice, we can get to the point where we don't even hear our conscience at all.

God gave us a conscience for a reason. Ignoring the conscience takes us down a deadly path strewn with failed relationships, hardship, and regret. We pave the road to silencing our conscience when we don't take responsibility for the wrongs we've done, flip the script, and make someone else responsible for what we've done. We point the finger at something they've done as a distraction tactic, or we justify our actions. Relationships need repair. Without repair we leave ourselves open to one of the other three broadcast voices: Society, Self, or Satan. Refusing to deal with issues leaves us open to our own insecurities or to the accusations of the enemy of our souls. When we have wronged someone, take my Mama Lee's advice, "Do right." What does that look like? Confess and ask forgiveness—the same that is required when we sin against God.

Here is a five-step tool to help people learn how to ask appropriately for forgiveness:
        1. Acknowledge/Admit

2. Empathize
3. Apologize
4. Ask Forgiveness
5. Amend

Most people start off by saying, "I'm sorry." This is often followed by a statement such as, "If I hurt/offended you in some way." How half-hearted is that? No one who has been hurt wants to hear the *if* word. Saying, "I'm sorry if I hurt you," is a cowardly way of not taking responsibility by masking it under an "I'm sorry." So what? What does your sorry do for me? Nothing. I'm still left with whatever you dropped into my life. You're probably just sorry that you were caught or sorry that you now have to deal with the conflict that came due to your actions, and you are looking for an easy way out by blurting out that you are sorry. Meanwhile, the offended person is left with whatever your actions brought to them.

In this five-step model, we want to begin an apology by naming what we did (Acknowledge/Admit). Another thing that often happens in apologies is we say we are sorry and when asked what we're sorry for, we can't name it. That's because we aren't connected to the wrong we've done. We are only saying we're sorry because either someone has asked for an apology, or we sense, due to barely tuned-into social cues, something is amiss, or we have done something wrong. Because we aren't really attached to the sin, we can't really be attached to the sorrow. In naming the wrong, we are admitting to what we did without requiring the offended person to have to explain why we owe them an apology. Acknowledging shows the offended person we have thought about our actions and have concluded that we need to do something about them. In other words, we're taking responsibility.

Let's use an example. Suppose you missed your close friend's fortieth birthday party because you had food poisoning. She is upset and she has told you she really wanted you there because that was a big birthday for her. Some people would feel justified in turning the tables on this friend because they should know you'd never miss an important event like that unless you had good reason. In this case, communication has gone astray. One person will bring an offense and desire to address it and the receiver of the communication makes it about them and decides to defend, justify, or make excuses instead of hearing the other person out.

Love requires that you hear out your loved one and put your own thoughts/feelings aside for the time being. When a person is hurt, either get into the hearing-them-out position or say nothing. Don't make it about you. When someone is hurt, she isn't thinking about what you meant. She is only thinking about what she experienced. At any rate, this is not the time to explain yourself. You aren't going to change her mind at this point anyway. Once good communication has been restored, she may be in a better position to understand what you meant. Why? Because she feels heard and she's better equipped to be in a receiving position. Now you are able to tell her your side of the situation. People aren't mind readers. Until both sides are heard, the full picture will remain unknown.

Back to our example:

Judy: "Why haven't you been returning my calls or answering my texts."

Carrie: "You flaked on my party."

Judy: (Acknowledging) "Oh. Yes. I did say I was going to come." It would be tempting to add a "but I was sick" here, but don't. Go into the next step of the process. After acknowledging, you want to move to step two and empathize by stating how you think it may have made the other person feel.

Judy: (Empathize) "My not being there must have made you feel disappointed and unacknowledged. Did you feel that way?"

Carrie: "Yes."

Judy: "Tell me more about that." Now listen. Let your friend tell you how she feels. Asking her how she feels builds empathy, and empathy is the ability to stand in the shoes of another, to feel what the other person feels. Trying to guess how she must have felt creates a dynamic that allows the person to sense, on a subconscious level, that you are trying to see the situation from her point of view. Empathy is especially effective if what you guess is actually how the other person feels.

Another reason you want to say "tell me more" is because it allows the other person to experience the psychological process of *catharsis,* which is the expression of thoughts and processing of feelings she may have been holding in after the event occurred. Think about it, how many conversations have you had in your head with yourself over someone who has hurt you? How many imaginary conversations have you had with that person in which you tell her off? Wouldn't it be nice to be able to just say what you need to say at the time of the event instead of carrying your negative feelings around for years, slowly and secretly poisoning the relationship and worse, poisoning yourself? Someone once said unforgiveness is like drinking venom and expecting the person you won't forgive to die.

Saying, "tell me more" gives the person permission to release whatever she is holding inside. This is good for the relationship, and it is also good for the person herself. While listening to the "more," don't interrupt, and again, resist the temptation to defend yourself. Mentally remind yourself this conversation is not about you. Even if you don't agree with what the person is saying, salvaging the relationship is more important. You can express your thoughts and feelings later, at a less intense moment, or you can choose to let it go, allowing things to rest with your friend's feelings expressed, if you know that part of what she is saying isn't who you are. You may have been the perpetrator of the disappointment, and that's something you have to accept because you brought it to the relationship. You can decide what you want to do with what she says at a later time, whether you want to change it or not. The call of the hour now is empathy and repentance. Repentance keeps the line to hearing God's voice clear. Repentance isn't just for sin; it's for any kind of change you want to affect.

Back to our example again.

After the person has expressed how she feels, then you want to say you are sorry. Notice the "I'm sorry" statement is three steps in, not number one. Although you are apologizing for the offense, you are also—and more importantly—apologizing for the rift in the relationship that the offense brought as well as the pain the person experienced. By now, the person has let out the attached feelings and may be more ready to accept your apology because your remorse is no longer about you.

Judy: (Apology), "I can see how much this has hurt you. I'm so sorry I missed the party."

Once you have that apology out, then you would move to step four in the process:

Judy: (Ask forgiveness), "Will you forgive me?"

Some people will readily forgive, as in this example, but some people may not be able to just yet. You may be met with a reply like, "Yes. I forgive you." The person may also say, "I don't know," "I need time," or "I'm not sure this is something I can forgive." Whatever the response, don't let the response dictate how you behave in the situation. Monitor and guard your heart against offense. No one owes you forgiveness anyway. Forgiveness is a gift.

On some occasions, once the person expresses how she feels and you apologize, she may say, "That's okay." If she says that, still continue to move through to step five to complete the process. Her saying it's okay. may be because it really is okay because she's talked it through. She may realize the offense wasn't as big a deal as she thought. Most likely, what helped her get there was the opportunity to process her thoughts and feelings in a safe manner without you justifying your own behavior. I've been in situations in which people just wanted to justify themselves. When they do this, they add insult to the injury they have already inflicted. Don't do it.

Wherever the person lands in her ability to forgive, you want to move on to step five.

Judy: (Amends), "What can I do to make this up to you, to make this right?" The person may state something you can do. If she does, carry out what she says as quickly as possible. Something has gone wrong in our culture where responsibility is not readily accepted even in the most harmful violations. On the other hand, the person may state she does not know what you can do. If that's the case, invite her to let you know when something comes to her mind and offer something to make up for the offense.

Let's say Carrie can't come up with something in the moment.

Judy: "Maybe I can take you to dinner? It can be just you and me, or we can invite Sarah and Parker if you like? On me, of course. We can call the dinner "Carrie's More Intimate Big 4-0."

For minor slights like if you forgot to take out the trash, just say you're sorry and take the trash out. This five-step model is for offenses that hurt or cause rifts. One last note about using this method. Though I've mentioned it above, I can't express it too much: you really want to guard against offense.

Know where you feel the tension of offense in your body: your head, throat, chest, gut, or hands. For most people, offense usually registers in one of these body parts. The purpose of getting in touch with where it registers in your body is training. Most people don't know they are offended until they react in offense with words or actions. When you train yourself to be mindful about what you're feeling physically, you more readily note what you are feeling emotionally. The problem with the onset of offense in conversations is it almost always causes us to defend ourselves. In the example above, if Judy would have defended herself, even though she really was sick—and even though Carrie may have known it or heard it through the grapevine—Judy's defending her position would not have allowed for the clearing of the disappointment Carrie felt from Judy's not being at her party.

A conversation such as this has a much better chance of processing feelings of hurt. Carrie may even say to Judy, "I heard you were sick so I know you wouldn't miss it on purpose." But for the sake of friendship and *thinking her friend better than herself*, Judy chose to hear her friend out even though she had a good reason for not attending that party. Philippians 2 admonishes us not to act out of vain conceit or selfish ambition.

By the way, although these steps are not required in the Bible, it wouldn't hurt to go through these steps when the Being you have offended is God. Admit what you've done, state how it must make Him feel, ask Him how He feels about it, listen for His answer, journal what comes to you, say you are sorry, ask forgiveness, and ask if there is anything you can do to make amends. It's not that we have to *make things up* to God. We don't. Jesus took care of all we owe. But it would be kind of you to offer restitution.

The importance of the relationship we have with Him exceeds the importance of the relationships we have with others. When you ask, He may have an idea. If He does, I bet whatever He asks of you would have more to do with you or with someone else He cares about in your life. Although He could ask for some alone time with you. For Him as with others, set aside time to make amends as soon as possible.

Now, let's unpack shame.

Chapter Eight
Hindrance #2: Shame

The second hindrance that can block our ability to hear from the Lord is shame. If you make a habit of going through the apology and asking forgiveness model mentioned with regard to your relationships, you will circumvent shame in many instances. Unlike guilt that tells us we did or said something wrong, shame tells us there is something fundamentally wrong with us. The focus of the problem shifts from the action to the individual.

But before we delve into shame and how it presents as a hindrance to belief in God and hearing from Him, let's look at some differences between shame and some of its cousins to dispel a few myths about them all being the same.

While people often use the words *guilt* and *shame* synonymously, humiliation and embarrassment are often swapped for these emotions as well. Guilt is the feeling that follows the idea, "I did something bad," while shame is the feeling that follows the idea, "I am essentially bad."

Embarrassment, often misinterpreted as either guilt or shame, is a brief or transient feeling that shows up when we do something that may make us blush, like tripping over our own feet or blurting out something without thinking. When we feel embarrassed, we know others have done this too. We don't think something is wrong with us, per se, and we don't necessarily think we've done something wrong. On some level, we know we've done something human that other humans all over the world have done, and we are able to let it go—perhaps even laugh at ourselves. Not so with shame. Shame is not transient, because whatever is occurring is defining us. We take shame in as evidence that we are bad.

Humiliation is also mistaken for shame at times. We experience humiliation when another person does something hurtful to us. Humiliation and shame are easily interchangeable, but they aren't the same thing. One way to differentiate what we are feeling is how we think about what has happened.

Let's say an employee is up for the *Person of the Department* award at work to be given at the next staff meeting. There are three departments, so each department nominates a person to win the award. At the meeting, four people are called up. Two of the departments simply called up the winner to announce them. One department, however, called up the winner and the runner-up, so now there is a public competition.

Only one of the last two standing is proclaimed the winner so there is only one of the four standing up there without their sad little globe.

This happened to me, by the way. I was the runner-up. Now, if my self-talk was "Darn, what a loser I am. What did I do wrong not to receive that globe? I never do anything right," then I'd be dealing with shame. *I believe I deserve the humiliation.* But if my thoughts leaned toward, *What the heck! Why didn't they just call up the winner like the other two departments? They had me standing up there like an idiot; the only one with no globe. These people! So disorganized*! Now I'm expressing humiliation. I felt humiliation because some of my therapist colleagues were smirking, looking as if they were thinking, "It must suck to be her right now." Also, I could read pity on some of their faces. And, I was the only one returning to my seat without a cotton-picking globe! See the difference? When humiliated, our self-talk will have us questioning others, not ourself.

Shame is debilitating to the human spirit and to relationships, especially our relationship with God. Since shame prevents us from believing what God says about us, making it difficult for us to believe anything good about ourselves. By the end of the chapter, we will have some understanding of shame and how detrimental it can be. First let's start with shame and the brain.

Your Brain on Shame

Scientists have found there is an intersection between neurobiology and shame. (1) At the start of the chapter, we talked a little about the differences between guilt, shame, humiliation, and embarrassment. Take that information and start to analyze yourself and your behaviors, teasing out the differences, so that you are no longer in the dark. Ask yourself, "Is what I feel guilt—because I've done something wrong, shame—because I believe something is wrong with me, embarrassment—because I just made a goof, or humiliation—because someone just did something to cause me shame or embarrassment? Checking in with yourself with questions such as these can help you find a way out of the debilitation that shame causes. Ultimately these questions can be used as tools against shame's ability to prevent you from hearing from God.

Even with the knowledge you gain from the above questioning process, it may be difficult to stop equating large, public events with shame when they are actually embarrassment or humiliation. Understand that shame occurs internally, for the most part. It comes from the thousands of conversations inside your head that say you are bad or unworthy.

If I were to sum up shame, I would say its ultimate purpose is to rob you of your identity. You are made in God's image, and you are worthy beyond measure. In God's eyes, you were worthy of Jesus' death on the cross. The Creator of the universe wants to be in close connection with you, for the sake of relationship, not for what He can get out of you. Contrary to what you may have been taught, His goal is not to inundate you with long lists of do's and don'ts that leave you feeling hopeless, as if you have to white-knuckle your way through life just to please Him to avoid hell.

Shame comes from Satan's voice, the Self voice, and the Society voice. If left unchecked, shame can destroy your sense of self, anything important in your life, and your relationship with your Heavenly Father. Satan is often at the helm of shame. He's still angry that he didn't win the revolt in heaven, that he still isn't sitting on the throne, and that he will never sit there. Anytime we rebel against God, though our rebellion will never give Satan the throne he covets, he does get to sit on someone's throne—the throne of your heart. So, in essence, he receives his ultimate wish, to be worshipped. He still doesn't win, per se, but you lose.

Satan will never stop trying to destroy your knowledge of who you are. He knows that if you don't know who you really are, you will spend a lifetime performing for approval, which is an attempt to get others to affirm what you'd like to think about yourself. If you only knew or sought to get in touch with who God created you to be, Satan's voice would become a mere echo, lost in the hills of your mind. He would never be heard again unless through sin, you invited him back into the village of your consciousness where he can wreak havoc once more.

Shame has an appetite that can never be satiated.

Once you are in the cycle of proving yourself through performance, performing will always be required of you.

Here are some ways you can identify and then dispel shame:

1. Investigate

Ask yourself, "Is what I am hearing/thinking a truth, a lie, or some form of insecurity?" Keep a notepad and write down the statements that come to your mind or type your responses into your phone. You'd be surprised how diligent shame can be. Be *more* diligent.

2. Banish Secrets

Shame festers in the dark. Vulnerability is the light that extinguishes the dark. In John 8:32, when Jesus said the truth will set you free, He wasn't just talking about the truth that He is the Savior of the world. He was speaking of truth in general. Being open can be risky, but openness offers a lifeline to freedom. Be honest with yourself and with God and consider talking to someone about what your mind is telling you to keep secret. Confession is cleansing to the soul.

3. Listen

When ridiculing yourself or making agreements with shame statements about who you are, ask yourself questions like, "What does God say about my identity in this moment?" Ask God, "Father, who do you say I am?" This question is a play on what Jesus asked His disciples. Peter answered correctly, and Jesus said Peter was blessed because the reply was given to him "by my Father in Heaven."

Jesus' Father in Heaven is your Father in Heaven too and will do the same for you if you only ask. You just have to take the time to listen for God's answer. Most of us are asking things of God throughout the day. We just don't sit quietly and listen long enough to receive His reply. The Lord commands us to be still in Psalm 46:10, and we need stillness for many reasons. One is so we can hear Him. It's not just because He wants you sitting still, although stillness and silence are marvelous for your brain and for warding off anxiety.

He wants you to sit still because it helps you cultivate that side of yourself that can hear Him, the side of yourself that you use to create the life He meant you to have.

It is important to use the three steps mentioned above to dispel shame. Shame twists who you are and prevents you from being who God made you to be. We originate from a creative God. Therefore, we have creativity inside of us. Shame blocks creativity and its life-giving force within us.

Shame and Creativity

Shame mercilessly attacks creativity. It lulls its victim into perfectionism, and perfectionism is like a noose around the neck of creativity. You can't move forward in any endeavor due to the feeling that what you have done is not good enough. Since shame doesn't allow you to feel secure in who you are, how are you going to feel secure about what you've created? In his book, *The War of Art*, author Steven Pressfield speaks of a phenomenon called *resistance*, which he describes as a force that opposes creativity and shackles the mind and will of creators across most artistic genres. (2) That definition resonates with me. When I sit down to write, the spirit of resistance is often right there to distract me to do something else—make a phone call, check email, fold laundry. Of course, when I give in to those urges, guess what happens? I feel guilty because I'd promised myself I would write that day. The guilt is followed by shame because I might tell myself I am a loser with no discipline, probably not even a real writer, and on and on.

That's the thing about shame; it gloms on to whatever is within its reach to use. Why am I talking about creativity? In all of the ways we are made in God's image, creativity is one of the most important parts of our identity. It keeps the human race going, and it brings beauty into the world.

Satan wants to kill all creativity in our lives.

Creativity is one of our spiritual connections to God. Why? Because it is the act of bringing something into being out of nothing.

Ask for God's Help

We don't have to wait until we get to heaven. Jeremiah 33:3 invites us to ask God questions. Asking God questions is a great way to hone-in on the frequency of the Savior's voice. As a spiritual practice, I like to sit and just listen to God. I'll ask a question, any question. Sometimes I ask spiritual questions, but most of the time the questions I ask would most likely be termed run-of-the-mill or conversational. The latter evolved as I habitually spent time in His presence. On some occasions, I would adhere to my plan of how I wanted to spend time with God, but on some occasions, when I didn't do what I'd planned, the spirit of resistance was probably the culprit, luring me away to distract me.

Being busy with distractions makes it hard to tune in to emotions of any kind. You still feel the emotions; you're just not aware that you feel them at the time. Underground emotions are more corrosive than the ones you know you have because in order to be regarded, they cause you to act out. I often encourage my clients to allow themselves to feel the emotions that surface, stating that feelings/emotions are like little children. They want to be acknowledged, and then they'll go on about their business. When we bury emotions, they prickle on the edge of consciousness. You may not say what you feel, or even allow yourself to be aware of what you are feeling, but in some way, your choices will show what you feel. When this occurs, unconscious choices lead straight to shame.

Isaiah 59 tells us that sin separates us from God. Shame has the potential to do the same thing. Don't let it. When you feel shame, acknowledge it, and explore the thought-source. Don't let shame distract you from dealing with what you are thinking. The distraction will only lead to silencing the Savior's voice and increasing the decibels of the Satan, Self, or Society voice, ultimately pushing you further from God and from truth.

Dissension

In one of my times of Bible study, I noted that God has a particular disdain for division and people who go about causing dissension (see Romans 16:17-18, Titus 3:9-11, Jude 1:16-19). I asked God, "Lord, I know you hate all sin, but the sin of dissension in all its forms seems to really bother you. Why is that?"

Before I could finish the sentence, what came to my mind was the answer, "Because it is what Lucifer did in heaven." Satan, whose name was Lucifer at the time, divided heaven by causing one third of the angels to go along with him in a coup attempt. He did it by lying to the angels. So, it is my guess that he keeps using what worked as he lies to you to riddle you with shame and move you away from the presence of God.

If you aren't in a person's presence, how do you think you will hear him? Don't get me wrong, the Bible says God will never leave nor forsake you. He doesn't. But we move away from Him mostly in thought and deed. It's kind of like when you are engrossed in something, like making dinner, but your mind is on a multitude of other things. You are monkey braining left and right, and your child comes in to tell you something. At first you tune in to acknowledge him because that's just how the brain works. It'll tune in to a new stimulus before reverting back to whatever it was previously engrossed in. The child starts to talk, and you listen for a minute or so, but then your mind is off to whatever it was flitting back and forth from before the child walked in. You haven't left the room, but you are no longer present with the child. You've moved away although the child is still physically in the room. In much the same way, God never leaves the room. Your mind just wanders off to other things. This takes us to the next hindrance: distraction.

Chapter Nine
Hindrance #3: Distraction

The third hindrance to hearing God's voice is distraction. Unfortunately, distraction has many tentacles and can present itself as mental, physical, spiritual, and obligatory preoccupation, stress, or clutter.

I'll start this section with an illustration. During the Second World War, the country needed secretaries to type up correspondence and messages to aid in the fight overseas. The manager of one firm, whose company was well-staffed, had a lot of business to attend to during a particularly busy season of the war. He felt he needed a secretary to take notes on and type up some of the issues that came across his desk, but he didn't want to detract from the pool of secretaries outside his door. The company and the country needed them to be where they were, so he decided to hire a personal secretary for special assignments.

He placed an advertisement in the newspaper and, it being wartime, about thirty-two young women applied. The pool hummed with typewriters whizzing and whirling out wartime correspondence. The applicants received instructions to fill out the application and wait in the noisy waiting room for their name to be called. The thirty-third woman walked in, picked up an application, and turned to face the other women crammed into the waiting area. She sighed as she saw all of the women with completed applications, all dressed to the nines, all waiting for their names to be called. She found a corner to lean into and started filling out her application. Midway through and fatigued from trying to write clearly while standing up, she paused to rub her neck. Glancing around the room, she suddenly stuffed the application and pen in her purse, strode past the receptionist, through the secretary pool and threw open the dark brown oak double doors at the other end of the room.

The other young women were all abuzz.

"Did you hear a name being called?"

"I didn't hear my name."

"I didn't hear any name."

"Maybe it's the typewriters."

"Should we ask the receptionist to ask them to keep it down?"

Panic quickly circulated, but no one made a move. They all waited to see what would happen next. About thirty minutes after the woman had marched into the office, she and the office manager walked out, all smiles, shaking hands.

"You can start tomorrow," he said.

"Thank you, sir. I will see you tomorrow."

The other applicants were more than miffed.

"What?"

"She was the last one here!"

"It's not fair that the rest of us, who were here before her, didn't even get an interview."

"I didn't even hear my name being called!"

"She can't just march in here and take a job!"

The office manager replied, "She didn't just take a job. She followed instructions." He pointed to several whiteboard posters that were on the walls, well within view of all areas of the waiting room. "These posters have a message that says, 'If you can read this, it means you know shorthand. Come straight into my office. The secretary job is yours.'"

How many of us are so distracted with what is going on around us that we miss the obvious? These young women were probably preoccupied with the noise of the typewriters, with their own nerves in wanting the job, and probably with who was wearing what and trying to figure out how they measured up to each other. Some probably didn't even read or know shorthand, so they were already unqualified. But back then, most secretaries did know shorthand. However, they were all so preoccupied with their own thoughts and with what was around them, they didn't notice the posters. The one who did, the one who tuned in, got the coveted position.

What could God be saying is yours, but you are too distracted to hear it because you're not tuned in to His voice? What prayers have you prayed that you are still awaiting an answer? What prayers have been answered but you're too busy to even notice? The Jews prayed for their Messiah, but when he came, they were too distracted by other things to notice He was right there in their midst. There was a lot going on at the time. They were under Roman rule, overtaxed, and surviving revolts and uprisings. It was stressful. This leads to another form of distraction, stress.

But before we get into stress, let's look at three tools to guard against preoccupation:

Decreasing Preoccupation

1. Finish what you start no matter how small.

Make it a habit to do one thing at a time. The myth of multitasking has been debunked in the world of neuroscience. The brain only focuses on one thing at a time. Can you actually have more than one thing going at a time? You can, but you won't do any of them well because you can only focus on one. What ends up happening is you get constantly distracted, moving from one thing to another without ever finishing the first thing you started.

2. Practice Mindfulness.

In some of the Christian community, mindfulness and meditation have received reputations as new-age practices that Christians should stay away from. But mindfulness and meditation were actually God's idea: Genesis 24:63, Deuteronomy 11:18, Psalms 77:11-12; 104:34; 119:15-16; and 143:5; Isaiah 26:3, (my personal favorite), Romans 12:2-3; and Colossians 3:2, just to name a few.

a. Mindfulness, in a nutshell, means what its name suggests: having our mind fully on what is happening in the moment. To meditate means to fix your mind on something in particular. Mindfulness and meditation keep you from ruminating on the past or worrying about the future. You are not your thoughts. You have control of your mind. You have the ability to decide what you will hold in your thoughts. Mindfulness and meditation teach you how to be a nonjudgmental observer of your thoughts. When your mind trails off, bring it back to the task or moment at hand. Second Corinthians 10:5 tells us we ought to capture our thoughts and make them obedient to Christ. Some of the medical benefits of taking captive your thoughts include:

i. Lower blood pressure
ii. Boosted immune system
iii. Reduced stress
iv. Reduced chronic pain
v. Reduced risk of heart disease

b. Breathe – Bringing your mind to the breath teaches you to bring your mind to right now. Becoming an observer of the moment decreases ego involvement. You are less likely to link your sense of self with the environment around you or with what others think. Becoming present through your breath allows you to accept the moment for what it is. You are less likely to associate whatever is happening around you as an extension of yourself.

c. Focus on how the air feels cool around your nostrils on the inhale and warm coming out on the exhale. Taking a breath and actually fixing your mind on that breath brings your mind to the right now in a way that prevents your mind from taking you captive. Stopping to take a breath is a reboot for your mind, so that you can respond instead of react. It gives you that beat you need. Practicing the art of mindfulness allows you to state: "This is what I am feeling. What thought am I having that is driving this feeling?" The thought you are having may be the meaning you are giving to the event that is unfolding in front of you. It is not the event itself. There is nothing that happens on the outside of you that can *make* you feel anything.

All three of these tools are right at your disposal in any given moment. All you have to do is choose to use them. To recap: Whatever you are working on, resist the urge to jump to the next task. Finish and then move. Though it is a good practice to carve out a time of mindfulness so that you can learn to cultivate the art of quiet and stillness, mindfulness can be practiced at any time. For example, if you're washing dishes, you can focus on how warm the water is, how fuzzy the suds feel, how the dishes sound as you place them on the rack. And since your breath is always right there with you, you always have access to this tool. Your breath is your best in-the-moment stress reducer.

Allowing yourself to be preoccupied increases your

stress level. I teach about the Stress Threshold which is the amount of stress any individual person can take before she reaches a limit that causes adverse reactions and behaviors. Stress thresholds can be reached because of burn-out, anger or hostility, vices, such as substance abuse, eating or sleeping too much or not enough, spending too much, isolation/withdrawal from people, and somatic symptoms of headache, stomachache, and other physical disturbances that do not have a medical basis. Stress is a strong hindrance to hearing God's voice because when people are in the throes of it, they dwell on how overwhelmed they are.

Decreasing the Distraction of Stress

Though often used in the same sentence or interchangeably, stress and anxiety are two distinct things. They go together, yes, but one is a physiological response to the other. Anxiety results from how we are thinking about what's going on, which will impact how we feel. It is a state of being ill-at-ease in one's mind. Stress, on the other hand, has more physical components because it can have some of the same components of a panic attack: racing heart rate, chest pain, a shift in our breathing, and sweating. Left unattended, the stress response can become a daily part of one's life. Imagine living in a state of panic from day to day! Yet, this is what we inadvertently sign up for when we don't get ahold of ourselves and our thoughts, when we don't tune out the noise and tune in to God.

It will take another book to delve into all that's involved with the management of stress, but for our present purposes, here are three ways we can push past stress to learn how to hear God's voice:

1. Release

Psalm 56:8 says God keeps track of our sorrows. He collects our tears and stores each one of them. I imagine He does this so we don't have to. Let Him have that which causes us sorrow. Give it over. The invitation is there waiting for us to accept. Releasing allows us to let go of things that are not within our control anyway, so allow God what, if anything, He wants to do with it.

2. Recycle

This is what we do after we release. Pray and ask God to take the circumstances and turn them into something useful for us, for the people we love, or for his Kingdom. A song lyric says, "You make beautiful things out of dust; you make beautiful things out of us." (1) This can be taken literally in that from the dust of the ground, God made man (Genesis 2:7 [KJV]. Or it can be taken figuratively to mean that when the dust settles from things blowing apart in our lives, God can turn that dust into something we never would have expected.

3. Relate

When the book of Isaiah says, "Incline your ear to hear," it is actually talking about an orientation of our hearts. Turn our hearts toward

God with the things that are causing us stress and anxiety. Turn to others as well. It is a good practice to learn who are the safe people in our lives. Safe people are those who will let us emote—get it all out—without feeling the need to correct us unless we ask for help.

Release, recycle, relate—doing these things will help us begin to meet ourselves where we are, know our place and God's, and let Him guide us to work out whatever is bringing stress into our lives.

The last distraction we will look at is clutter. We will examine four different kinds of clutter: mental, physical, spiritual, and obligatory.

Mental Clutter

First up on the list is mental clutter. These are the old ideas that have nothing to do with who we are now or where we are currently going. This clutter masquerades as negative thoughts, regrets about the past, and fears about things that probably won't ever happen. Mental clutter contains thoughts from the land of what-if that came to visit and took up permanent residence in our minds. If we give airtime to what used to be, we can't enjoy now, and we certainly won't be attuned to what is to come. God speaks in a still small voice. If we are attached to thoughts of regret or who we used to be, not forgiving ourselves, others, and our past, we will be greatly hindered from becoming who God made us to be.

Jesus didn't just save us for the afterlife. He saved us so that we can have a great, productive life in this one as well (John 14:12).

There are three aspects of salvation in theological terms: justification, sanctification, and glorification. *Justification* is the salvation of our souls. This happens as a result of our good confession. When we accept that Jesus died on the cross, was buried and rose again, we are freed from the penalty of sin. This freedom is not something earned. We can't do anything to be justified. Jesus completed the work on the cross. All we have to do is believe and accept. Sometimes we'll hear people jokingly say, "I've been saved many times," referring to the process of being saved by entering into God's light and His kingdom. Justification through salvation here on earth is a one-time event.

Then there is *sanctification*. Sanctification happens throughout our lives. In short, God had a certain someone in mind when He created each of us. Sin, life's circumstances, bad choices, grief, and other things contort us into someone we were never meant to be. Sanctification is the process that corrects that. It is the process by which we are being transformed into Christ's likeness (2 Corinthians 3:18).

Our journey gets us lost in more ways than one. Sanctification peels all the layers off to take us back to our original design. We each reflect Him in our own unique way.

Sanctification is also at play all our lives because

although we have been freed from the penalty of sin, we still have to battle the sinful side of ourselves. The Bible says we have a sin nature. It's the side of ourselves that misses the mark, and in some cases the side of ourselves that wants to miss the mark. The "mark" is God's standard for our lives (John 3:19-20). Sin causes spiritual deformity, while sanctification restores the beauty God intended for us.

Glorification is what happens on the other side of this life. It's the point at which we are no longer in the presence of sin. During the sanctification process, and after justification, sin is present and always will be.

In Genesis, God told Cain, right before Cain killed his brother Abel, that sin was crouching at his door desiring to have him. What a warning! God went so far as to personify sin to let Cain know what he was up against. Cain killed his brother even after God told him about that war within. In Cain's case, most scholars believe it was the sin of envy that drove him to do what he did. Maybe it was. Maybe Cain's envy arose from a disbelief in himself, a disbelief that God could change his heart, or a belief that God loved Abel more. He may have thought his brother had it easier. Not being able to stand looking at his brother, he killed him. This is, of course, conjecture to demonstrate how we allow our minds to perseverate on the outside instead of looking at what is inside ourselves.

For the purpose of our exploration, we don't have to worry too much about the glorification process because sin is no longer "crouching at our door." At this point we've slid across home base.

Decreasing Mental Clutter

This is the point of discussing these three aspects of salvation: Mental clutter keeps us distracted from the here and now. Jesus is "the same yesterday, today and forever," says Hebrews 13:8 (NIV). We need to focus our attention on today. What is going on now? Our today will impact our tomorrow. Many people allow the past to take away the joy of today and steal their future from the plans God has for them.

Here are three ways to get rid of mental clutter as it relates to our past:

1. Recognize that life is a journey.

Sometimes mistakes are a necessary part of our growth process. When we can look to who we were or what we did in order to see how it helped form who we are now, we can accept our journey for what it is. Some of the mistakes we made may not have been necessary, but there isn't anything we can do about it. So, we move forward.

2. Forgive ourselves.

God has. Acknowledge what we have done. Talk with God about it and ask pardon. Then pardon ourselves. Realize that the past can be a learning experience if we let it. Let go of what we have done and resolve to do it no more.

3. Seek professional help.

Go see a therapist or speak with a pastoral counselor to gain an understanding into why these tapes are playing in our head. Gather tools for cognitive restructuring to help restructure our thoughts in a way to release ourselves from mental images that are not serving our journey.

Physical Clutter

The second kind of clutter is *physical clutter*. This is stuff we have lying around in disarray. Things that need to be stored or given away. Things that need to be cleared out are just trash masquerading as clutter. Throw it away. The amount of energy it drains when we have to look at it all the time is not worth the trouble. If we find it difficult to declutter, consult an expert or find free advice on someone's YouTube channel. Physical clutter has an impact on our minds and our emotions, so it tends to eat up more space than is actually seen.

Decreasing Physical Clutter

Three ways to get rid of physical clutter:

1. The one-third principle
Consider making decluttering a personal act of worship. Determine to go through your stuff and give away one third of it once a year. One of my professors in grad school at Azusa Pacific University, Professor Tisdale, shared with us that she did this. Once a year, she would go

through all of her belongings and sacrifice one third of her things: shoes, clothes, kitchenware, and gadgets. She'd started it as a spring-cleaning tool and came up with the idea to give her things to the poor as a personal act of worship. It wasn't always easy, she admitted, but she did it anyway. After a while, her ritual became something she looked forward to. Since she turned it into a personal act of worship, it brought her closer to God.

A variation of this exercise is for one week, decide on three to five items you will give away. Each day, put your items in a box that you will donate at the end of the week. On Friday or Saturday, drop off the box at The Salvation Army, Goodwill, or your local domestic-violence shelter. Another variation of the one-third principle can be to adjust the number to one tenth. Turn your clearing out into a tithing principle, and give away one tenth of your goods.

2. Take a look at your kitchen

Identify which foods have expired and throw them away. Perhaps identify which foods are contaminating your body like processed foods, sugary snacks, or unhealthy things and replace those with healthy alternatives.

3. Before purchasing, give it a day

One of the well-known decluttering experts advises that when you are clearing out your stuff, hold it in your hand, and ask yourself if it brings you joy. (2) If not, put the item in throwaway or giveaway piles. I would advise this tactic when you are thinking of making a purchase as well. Hold it, and then put it back on the rack. Decide whether or not you, a) need it or b) really want it. The reason you should give it a day is because when you hold it in the store, it probably will bring joy. Making purchases releases endorphins and other happy hormones in your brain. So, in the moment, the happiness you feel will convince you to go ahead and buy the item. If you give yourself a day, you may be able to recognize that the thing you wanted was merely triggering a dopamine boost that doesn't bring true happiness.

Spiritual Clutter Defined

The third type of clutter is spiritual. What I am referring to as spiritual clutter is the man-made edicts, beliefs, and rules that Christian people put onto other Christian people as a way to control their walk with Christ, maintain an image, or keep the peace. It makes me think of what Jesus referred to when He accused the Pharisees and scribes of putting difficult burdens on people's shoulders that were too hard for them to carry.

Common Examples of Spiritual Clutter

Seven examples of spiritual clutter:

1. Christians don't get depressed.
Truth: When certain symptoms, (sadness, isolation, change in sleeping, etc.), show up

together, depression occurs. Depression is the brain's chemical reaction to those symptoms. Depression is also the heart and soul's long-term—two weeks or more—response to thoughts showing up as a result of whatever is going on in the person's life. Since Christians have brains and hearts, they can also have depression.

2. Anxiety is practical atheism because God is in control.

Truth: Anxiety is primarily caused by thought patterns, and it can also be caused by brain chemistry. The fear that accompanies anxiety can be a symptom of momentarily forgetting that God is in control, but it is not proof that a person does not believe in God. Atheism is a belief that there is no God. People who believe there is a God and claim Christ as their personal Savior are not atheists. Christians can become anxious because Christians have worries and fears. Because anxiety is, in essence, a fear-based disorder, anyone trapped in thought patterns that produce fear of any kind can develop anxiety. That includes Christian people.

3. If you were spiritual, you wouldn't still be grieving.

Truth: Grief is a response to loss. When people lose someone they love or something important to them, the natural response is grief. Experiencing grief has nothing to do with spirituality. Some of the people who would have received a diagnosis of grief in the Bible include:

a. <u>Joseph's Brothers</u> – Genesis 45:3-5 – Joseph's brothers were grieved about what they had done to him when they found out how mighty Joseph was in the land of Egypt. When they sold him into slavery, they had no idea that one day they'd be facing famine and standing before the brother they wronged, asking for relief and deliverance.

b. <u>Hannah</u> – 1 Samuel 1:6-7 – Hannah felt misery because she didn't have children, and her husband's other wife, who had many, kept throwing it in her face. In Hannah's culture, it was considered a curse not to be able to have children. Another predecessor to grief is when one doesn't understand why something is happening to them. Hannah was a prayer warrior, devoted to God. She didn't understand why God wouldn't give her this blessing of all blessings. The result was sadness accompanied by a refusal to eat. Hannah's husband didn't help the situation. He tried. It didn't help when he said, "Don't I mean more to you than ten sons?" His saying this to her probably caused more grief.

c. <u>Jonathan</u> – 1 Samuel 20:30-34 – Jonathan was grieved about his father's intention to kill David to make sure Jonathan's reign on the throne would be established. Jonathan's dad, Saul, was the most powerful man in the realm. I imagine Jonathan thought David was as sure as dead if his dad wanted it so. He warned David to run, and in doing so, he figured he'd never see his best friend again. Either way Jonathan would lose David, either in death or in separation, so he grieved.

    d.   <u>Jesus' Disciples</u> – Matthew 17:23 – The disciples had grief when they learned Jesus was going to be betrayed and killed. They loved Him and knew He was a good leader. They couldn't understand why anyone would want to kill Him.

    e.   <u>Jesus Himself</u> – Matthew 26:37-38 – Jesus had a lot of sorrow over what was about to happen to Him. Though obedient to God, it seems He had trepidation about going to the cross. He prayed to God asking Him to take away the cup. I wonder if, in His grief in the garden, whether the *cup* Jesus was asking about included the grief and anxiety over the pain and torture He was going to suffer. I wonder if it wasn't just about going to the cross as some scholars point out. Jesus was obedient to God, even to death on the cross, so what if He was actually praying for strength to endure what He had taken on to Himself, and not for God to change His mind about Jesus doing this?

Some scholars say it was the human side of Jesus that changed His mind about going to the cross. Maybe that's true. But maybe it's also true that it was the human side of

Him that needed the strength to endure what was to come? At any rate, the New Testament shares many instances of Jesus' grief and sorrow. The Garden of Gethsemane was one of the biggest examples.

    f.   <u>God Himself</u>! – Genesis 6:6 talks about God being sorry He made man because of all the evil in man's heart. He didn't just regret making man; He had sorrow and anguish (alternate words for grief). God was grieved several times throughout the Old Testament over several disappointments brought on by His people.

4. Once an addict, always an addict.

I've worked with Christians who have had struggles with alcohol, for example, are told not to attend weddings unless the planners agree not to serve alcohol because the presence of alcohol will make them struggle. Truth: What we struggle with is not the bride's or groom's issue. One person's problem is that person's problem. If the rest of the world had to adjust itself for other people's problems, this would be an entirely limiting place. No one would be at peace. No one would have joy. Life would be one big practice in the art of walking on the eggshells of other people's issues.

In the wedding example, the wedding day is special for the couple. It is special for others as well, but what is served and not served should not be dictated by someone else's addiction. The couple can decide on their own not to serve alcohol, but to demand it so they can be honored by our presence is ridiculous. Stay home. Some people have to decide to stay away from alcohol, period. That's a personal choice that should be made by that person, based on their relationship to the substance. That's fine. But to identify ourself as less than what God created us to be is damaging overall.

God didn't create us to be addicts but at the same time, God says to cut out things that cause us to stumble so there is a balance. If we stumble because of the substance, then it should be cut out. We are not our predilections. It's not so much the alcohol or the drug that is the problem. We should examine how we think about ourselves and the role we assign to the substance abused.

I'm not encouraging someone who has twenty-five years of sobriety to go out and have a drink. We are learning about beliefs and how we think. I'm talking about not thinking of ourself as 'less than' because we've identified ourself as an addict for twenty-five years. Alcohol abuse is a problem a person may have, it is not the person they are. We are to remain on the journey to becoming who God created us to be. For some, that may mean never touching a substance because of who it recreates them to be. In the process of this, know that substance or not, we are image bearers of the One True and Holy God.

5. "To be equally yoked, you would have to only date or marry someone from *this* church."

Truth: Second Corinthians 6:14 could require a book on its own because while equally yoked can apply to marriage, it can also be applied to attachment to people in a variety of areas that will only bring misery. For example, it is important to be equally yoked with people in business, sharing a dwelling, hobbies and sports, because we are working toward the same goal. With regards to marriage, though, being equally yoked is important because when people aren't married to someone of the same faith, issues like premarital sex, tithing, and values can pose problems. Marriage can be more difficult than it has to be if we are not in agreement in these areas. Being unequally yoked can cause us to compromise our beliefs and how we live out our walk with God. We can also be pulled away from our beliefs altogether. I had a friend who grew up in a Baptist church. She married a man who wasn't a Christian. He had some strong ideas about the crucifixion. He didn't believe it occurred in order to save our souls. He contended that Jesus was a rebel who was leading a revolt, and because He broke the law, His punishment, like others punished in that day for revolt, was crucifixion. While it's true that Jesus was seen as a rebel, God already had a plan of salvation that revolved around Jesus being the sacrificial lamb, crucified on the cross. See Psalm 34:20, Isaiah 53:7, and 12, and Zechariah 11:12-13. My friend's husband believed Jesus' crucifixion had nothing to do with us. Guess what? My friend eventually believed the same thing. After his many convincing talks with her, his arguments eventually made sense.

Second Corinthians talks of coming out and being separate from those who do not belong to God. However, people in other churches, unless they haven't received the gift of salvation, generally do belong to God. I too would advocate that Christian people marry other believers because of what this Scripture says, but I would not go so far as to say that only the people who sit under the same physical steeple as I sit are the only ones saved.

6. Only extroverts are spiritual people. Being an introvert is selfish. To avoid this, you have to be out of yourself to be considered giving.

Truth: Whether a person is an extrovert or an introvert indicates a preference that person has for social situations. It is a personality trait, not a spiritual characteristic. The personality God gave you is best suited for helping you achieve the things God created you to do in this life.

Extroverts are energized in the presence of other people. Introverts recharge in smaller groups or alone. The latter doesn't mean selfishness any more than the former qualifies a person as unselfish.

Some people who are extroverts can often be described as attention-seeking, which means they are getting something from being around others. This is not necessarily giving. Some people who are introverts can be described as thoughtful and reflective which means in conversation, they are more likely to take care when sharing thoughts and feelings rather than, in the name of truth, thoughtlessly blurting out things that hurt others. Of these two descriptions, which would more likely carry the moniker, "spiritual"?

7. It is spiritual to give advice.

Truth: It is not. Pushing one's opinion on others is not spiritual; it's a boundary violation. The Bible says it is righteous to seek advice. That's not the same thing as giving unsolicited advice. Someone sharing a problem with a person is not equivalent to an invitation for that problem to be solved by the person listening. Also, people aren't always looking to be fixed. Offering unsolicited advice can send the message that we think of the person speaking as broken or defective. If the person reaches out for advice, then she has recognized a need on her own. She is using her resources to find help by seeking it out. In short, the practice of giving unsolicited advice creates spiritual clutter in our heart that produces self-righteousness. Clear out the spiritual clutter to make space for hearing from God.

These examples are often rooted in opinion, church culture, and leadership preferences. At times they are a focus on external behavior, both of which are fueled by fear as a root rather than love as a basis. In essence, spiritual clutter is anything that requires you or anyone else to live in impossible ways without the leading of the Holy Spirit. Any requirement that is not backed up by scripture can be spiritual clutter when its burdensome. Anything that puts you in a position to please man over obedience to God is spiritual clutter. Thoughts and ways of being we are holding onto in an effort to prove we are saved is spiritual clutter.

Decreasing Spiritual Clutter

Here are three tips for getting rid of spiritual clutter:

1. Consult the scriptures on any edict, belief, or rule that gives you pause or causes your gut to wrench. If it aligns with the Bible, ask the Holy Spirit to help you do what you cannot do on your own, and be obedient.
2. Take the advice to two or three people who know you. Run your situation by them and ask if it sounds like something you should do, given their knowledge of you. It may be a good idea to run it by someone who isn't part of your

immediate church circle—someone from a different congregation, who you know to be solid in their faith, full of wisdom, and with a firm understanding of God's Word.

3. Take unsolicited advice and ask God if that advice was from Him. Set it aside if you have the sense it is not. If the advice is something you need to hear, it will come back to you. Discard it if God tells you it is not from Him. And discard any guilt associated with discarding it.

Obligatory Clutter

The fourth type of clutter is obligation.

My definition of obligation here is whatever you have said yes to and placed on your calendar, as well as things you have agreed to do. Requests that will eat up your time or that has not been placed on your schedule are not obligations. Before saying yes to anything, ask the person for their deadline and look at your schedule. If you have free time, ask yourself if you want to use your time doing what they've asked and then decide on your answer.

Obligation could also be classified as a distraction. While this is true, in regard to learning how to tune in to God's voice, obligation runs a little deeper than offering distraction. A packed schedule can easily appear to beef up our spiritual or egotistical resume.

"What a good mom I am! I'm driving my kids back and forth from sun-up to sun-down. Whew, when will I ever get a moment for myself?"

When we come from this perspective, we may as well rest the back of our hand against our forehead and pretend to *get the vayp-uhs!* We're not fooling anyone but ourselves.

"My ministry would just implode without me. I mean, it's like my hand has to be in every single thing that needs to be done. I wish I could clone myself."

"This company depends on me. I have to be at every meeting, make every conference, be the first one to arrive and the last one to leave."

While filling up our schedule with obligations will definitely prevent us from tuning in to God's voice, it will also have us perpetually tuned in to the voice of Satan, Society, or Self. Filling up our schedule is often tantamount to running ourself in the ground. No matter how much we try, with Satan and with our own ego, there is never enough. The inability to say no is a sign of people-pleasing. We don't think we are good enough, or we subscribe to the works mentality of earning the salvation that's already been given to us. Becoming trapped in these kinds of thoughts about ourselves keeps us from being tuned in to where we need to be.

Decreasing Obligatory Clutter

Earlier in the book, I discussed the spirit of Root, whose job is to distract you from who you truly are by taking who God meant you to be and telling you that you are something or someone else. The spirit of Root lies. It will say that you need to be perfect and then say you're falling short. Or when you are good at something, it will convince you that you are no good at whatever it is you're are embarking on. It's also likely to tell you that you're being selfish by spending so much time on what you love. The spirit of Root uses a packed schedule to trap people on the hamster wheel.

Here are some tips for decluttering your mind and calendar from obligatory clutter:

    1. Priorities List

List your priorities for the day. You can do this daily: first thing in the morning, the end of the day before you shut down work, or as part of your evening routine. Or you can make it a fifteen to twenty-minute habit once per week to write out what you want to accomplish over the next week, and then assign a set of priorities that match what you'd like to accomplish to each day.

    2. If something falls outside of those priorities, either let it go, delegate, or give yourself permission to address it at a later time. The planner (calendar) industry has a wide variety of options that will allow you to write out your plan for how you use your time. When you use your time to engage in behaviors that do not align with your priorities, you feel heavy-hearted, angry, and stressed. Manage your "yes."

Only say yes to things that fall under your priorities category. This prevents you from filling up your calendar with mediocre events and acquiescing to other people's priorities. Honoring your commitments to what you have prioritized can be a deflection against people-pleasing.

3. Core Relationship Assessment

Ask yourself whether or how saying yes will impact your core relationships. While almost anything you say yes to will have an impact on the core people in your life, evaluating how and to what extent those people are impacted will help you in your decision of whether to pass. Sometimes, people say yes to things because of guilt. Busying yourself can become a form of penance. If there is a sin in your life you may unconsciously think that saying yes is a way for you to clear yourself. It is not. Whatever needs clearing, confess, repent, receive forgiveness, and "sin no more."

Chapter Ten
<u>Hindrance #4 – Fear</u>

The final hindrance to belief in what God says is fear. This one is extremely important because fear competes for your attention; it comes from the Satan voice. However, we will focus on fear as a hindrance to hearing God's voice.

In his song "Stop This Train," John Mayer says, "Fear is a friend who's misunderstood." (1) Fear is an emotion that is and has been necessary for our surviving certain situations. If you see a snarling dog, fear prevents you from venturing near that dog. When contemplating walking down a dark alley alone at night because it is a shortcut, fear of who may be in the dark prevents you from going down that path. When recognizing you are on a certain life path and you need to turn around, fear of the consequences of what can happen if you don't cause you to make the necessary changes. For example, you may decide to change your career because the stress associated with the work will eventually lead to illness or death. Or you might change your diet because of fear of how the way you currently eat is negatively impacting your health.

However, fear that debilitates rather than prompts you into positive action is the fear that becomes a problem. Fear can impede areas of your life in which you should move forward. Fear should not hinder you in areas such as your career, your relationships with others, your relationship with God, or your goals.

A quick google search reveals that the phrase "fear not" is used in the Bible anywhere from 80 to 365 times. That last number is poetic since we have 365 days of the year. It would be just like the Father to warn us against fear every day. Not only does He warn us, but each of those "fear nots" is a command. What God commands is for our good, not necessarily His. There's a reason for the command that is designed to protect, serve, or help us live how we are meant to so that we walk in all He has for us. What God has for us is for us. But we get in our own way.

Let's hypothesize on how this could look once we reach heaven. The following is based on a story by Bruce Wilkerson that someone once sent me in one of those "think about it" emails. (2) To emphasize the point of why we shouldn't allow fear to block our blessings, I am elaborating on the story:

A woman dies and goes to heaven. Jesus is giving her the grand tour of the mansion that is set aside for her. He may say, "And this room has been apportioned due to your love of aircraft. In here you can continue to fly planes you loved to fly during your time on Earth, but to a much more amazing degree."

"My, my," says the woman, "I certainly look forward to that. Can I fly family members?"

"Yes," Jesus replies, "the members who are here and the ones who will soon be joining you."

This goes on for several rooms of the tour. At the turn of one corner, the woman notices a room with a white door and a golden bolt blocking its entrance. "What's in there?" she asks.

"Oh, you don't want to know. It's not important at this point." Taking the woman's arm, Jesus redirects her to the next room where she can climb any mountain she had her heart set on climbing while she was on Earth. The woman had managed to climb a couple of small mountains while on Earth.

After viewing this room, the tour again leads them past the bolted door. Once more, she asks what is behind the door, and again, Jesus redirects her attention, only this time, she isn't as easily distracted. Her gaze lingers over her shoulder before she turns to follow Jesus.

As they continue through the mansion, she becomes more and more excited about the features of the rooms the Father had prepared for her. But by the third time they pass the bolted door, the woman insists that she see what is behind it.

"Not that I'm ungrateful, Lord, but I simply can't live

here in peace, seeing that door and never knowing what is behind it."

Jesus sighs. "Well, if you must. But I have to tell you, no good will come of you seeing behind that door. It never does for anyone who insists on opening it."

"Then why is it here?"

"Because it is yours. What the Father has prepared for you, He has prepared for you."

"Then I for sure want to know what's in there," she exclaims. "It doesn't make any sense for me to deny what the Father wants to give me. Why should I settle for less?"

Again, Jesus sighs and states, "As you wish."

They approach the door. The woman grins, anxious to walk inside.

Jesus says, "Okay, lift the bolt. It is after all your door."

The woman eagerly lifts the bolt and swings the door wide. Purposefully stepping inside, she is immediately perplexed.

"What the—?" She turns to Jesus.

Jesus wags His finger. "Ah, ah, ah, not here," He playfully admonishes.

The woman turns back to the room, eyes wide, jaw hanging. It's filled, floor to infinite ceiling, with white boxes. All shapes and sizes. Tall ones, skinny ones, fat ones, short ones, ones that seem to take up the space of half a football field!

Turning to Jesus the woman confesses, "I am at a

complete loss. What is all this?"

Jesus answers, "These, dear heart, are all the gifts the Father desired you to have on Earth."

The woman walked over and opened one shaped like an envelope. Inside were airline tickets to Japan. She'd always wanted to go to Japan to climb Mount Fuji. She'd wanted it to be a trip she took with her husband, but she always made excuses: Not this year. Now is not a good time for that kind of expense. The memory of those excuses ring in her head as she stares down at the two tickets in her hand. Turning to Jesus she shakes her head. "Why would God deny me this experience?"

Jesus replies, "Did *He* deny you, or did you deny yourself?"

The woman is too embarrassed to reply, though she knows the answer. Jesus fills her in anyway.

"Again, what is yours from the Father, is yours. These are the gifts you desired but were too afraid to ask for. You thought you weren't good enough to receive these gifts and you thought you had to work to earn them. You were the only block to the full life your Father in heaven had planned for you. The Father sent Me to prepare the way for you to have all of these."

The woman begins to cry. "Please," she pleads. "Please let me go back and warn my family so when they get here, they won't have to see their version of this room!"

Jesus replies, "Not possible. Besides, even if someone returned from the grave to tell them that life is for the living, their fears will still convince them to play it safe, settle, and wait for just the right moment, which I and you now know, will never come. They have a manual, and though those who make it here listen to and follow much of that manual, the passages pertaining to life to the full are largely ignored."

The woman hangs her head. She admits, "You're right. Most of them, myself included, are waiting for when they get to heaven to experience true joy." She places the tickets back into the envelope and puts it back on the shelf where she found it. "Is it possible to have this room hidden from my sight somehow? I don't want a constant reminder of what I could have had, done, or been while I had my time on Earth."

"As you wish," Jesus replies. With a wave of His hand, the door and the room behind it disintegrate down to a sparkly speck of dust and then disappear from their sight altogether. As an added gift, Jesus touched the left temple on the side of the woman's head to erase the memory of what she'd just seen. After all, heaven is really no place for regret.

This story is an illustration of how fear holds us back in our relationship with God, not only in relating to Him one-on-one, but in receiving all He has for us. Fear serves many purposes that go against what God intended. Fear is exemplified by the following:

- A weapon used by Satan (1 Peter 5:8)

- A weapon people use against themselves and others to block true vision (Proverbs 29:18)
- A weapon used to diminish our hope (Isaiah 35:4)
- A weapon used to limit our victories (Psalm 118:6-7)
- A weapon used to shut our voices (2 Chronicles 15:13)
- A catalyst that causes us to forget our standing with God (Isaiah 43:1-3)
- A catalyst to cause us to settle and become comfortable in a way that leads to apathy (Jeremiah 29:11 and Revelation 3:16)
- A weapon used to cause us to give in to sin (Luke 23:34)
- A weapon used to make us take short cuts (Luke 9:62)
- A weapon used to keep us from doing the good we ought to do (James 4:17)

The list can go on for pages. Fear also causes hate, not only of others, but of oneself. Just look at the social and racial injustice that has occurred in our own country over hundreds of years. Much of those injustices are caused by fear. People often do not just hate the race of people they target. Much of that hate is self-loathing disguised as racism, a projection of what one feels about oneself.

People say hate is the opposite of love. I think fear, and specifically self-fear, is the opposite of love. Hate is a by-product of self-fear. We fear who we really are. This creates this elemental of self-fear. After years of being told that we are not enough, the part of our brain that believes this comes in direct conflict with the part of ourselves that does not believe it. There is a part of us that doesn't buy into the belief that we aren't good enough. It's the part that has been told otherwise or that has had experiences that suggest otherwise. In the end, what we believe about ourselves boils down to the idea of the two dogs in the backyard. The one you feed is the one that grows. In applying the interventions in this book, you are feeding the dog that will help you cultivate a mind that believes what God says about you.

For too long, this emotion of fear that was meant for our good has ultimately been used to prevent our good, our growth, and our progress in life. In the song mentioned above, after John Mayer says that fear is a friend who's misunderstood, he follows with, "I know the heart of life is good." God and His ways are our heart of life. God is good. Peace. He is holy. He is time immeasurable. An eternal Being who created us, His children, to dwell with Him eternally. We all want to go home. But we have to follow His voice. To be at home with Him now in our hearts, we have to stop and listen, or at least develop a habit of slowing down from time to time to listen. We have to tune into the broadcast voice that leads us home.

This reminds me of *I Am Legend*, a movie starring Will Smith. (3) In it, Smith's character seems to be the sole survivor of a zombie apocalypse. Seemingly, all of the people who weren't killed were turned into zombies by a new medication that was supposed to cure cancer. Somehow, Smith was immune to it and survived. He learned about the zombies and how to live among them by avoiding them, living in a tightly shut haven by nightfall. During the day he would forage for supplies. He would also go down to a warship in the harbor and broadcast a message to anyone listening, stating he had food and supplies. Anyone in need who could hear his voice was welcome to come and join him. He had faith that someone else out there had survived and wanted to connect with them. He was willing to give them what they would need.

God is the same way. He broadcasts to our hearts on a daily basis, calling all of us home. And He calls not just people who do not have faith; He's also broadcasting to the saved. Baptism and salvation do not clear your thought life. The faith to accept Jesus' invitation saves, but we still have to journey through life.

Fear is a hindrance because it makes us forget what we have at our disposal. It makes us forget what we want for our life. Wholly and willingly surrendering to God requires boldness, because to do so requires your turning your back on fear, the way of self, and enticements to go the way of destruction.

Claiming what is rightfully yours requires boldness. Courage is action in the face of fear. Boldness is an absence of fear. If you belong to God, you have this boldness. You just may not be aware that you have it due to being told otherwise or due to experiences that say otherwise. Develop a practice that allows boldness to operate inside of you. Be "Bold as Love," as the Jimi Hendrix song suggests. (4) Jimi was as bold as love. The dude went for it with his music. Isn't it interesting how people who operate within their God-given original design are often either cut down short in life or are targeted by others who wonder, "Who does this person (freak) think they are to be living boldly?" A question like this is the problem of the person asking, not yours. Being seen as an oddball may feel uncomfortable and lonely at first. With God's help, you'll make it through. Don't give up.

Understand this: feeling *weird* is sometimes a projection from other people. If you are living boldly, they know on some level that they should be too. Your decision to live in accordance with who God made you to be may bring up feelings of discomfort in someone who isn't. They can either decide to address this within themselves or not. Unfortunately, that's a high road some people aren't even aware they need to take, so they dismiss whatever is coming up for them by projecting that discomfort onto you. The more you walk in all that God has for you, the more fearlessly you'll live because you are operating according to your original design.

Yeah, people who go against the grain are often considered "strange" or "unusual" or even "dangerous" because they refuse the status quo. A description of *Bold as Love's* theme on Wikipedia states it as a "battle of passions" with the conclusion being that if you are going to be involved, love requires hard work and commitment.

Part Three:
The Strengthened (Soaring Identity)

Chapter Eleven
Be Still and Know That He is God
Tools to Stay Tuned In to the Savior's Voice

Throughout the chapters of this book, you have received tools to help you on your journey of developing a stronger belief or help you choose whom you will believe. In this chapter, I want to offer you tools on how to stop listening to the noise of Self, Satan and Society, and start listening to the voice of the Savior. Though the mind can jump from topic to topic in rapid succession, it has to land on one thought at a time.

Spending time with God will give Him greater influence in your life and how you see the world. Prayer is communication with God, and it can be an active part of your life. That is what Paul meant in 1 Thessalonians 5 when he said to "pray without ceasing" (ASV). The Greek translation of "without ceasing" means continually or without intermission, but many Bible translations (for example, the NIV), translates the verse to say, "Pray continually." The way I conceptualize what Paul says here is for us to make prayer an active part of our life; maybe, in much the same way as talking with a loved one.

In order to hear the Savior's voice, we must turn off the voices that compete with God's, tune into God's voice, and turn off the noise in our heads from other people. People often use the scripture about "working out your salvation in fear and trembling" in order to breed a works-oriented mindset into us and induce us to do what they think we ought to do instead of what God actually says to do.

I have always been a believer in Christ. As mentioned before, I grew up Catholic. We were so Catholic; one church wouldn't do. We attended Our Lady of Grace, which was the small church up the street most Sundays. Our other church home was St. Jude, which was the church my grandparents belonged to when they lived in New Orleans. Although they had moved to a small town about twenty miles outside of New Orleans, for over thirty years, they still trekked out to St. Jude for special occasions. As a member of two Catholic churches, I learned early on about the identity of the Father, the Son, and the Holy Ghost. Prayer was always front and center in our family life. My grandmother would require weekly family prayer times. Even aunts who no longer lived at home would come for these gatherings.

Unfortunately for me, I conceptualized prayer as

something I owed God, something I had to check off my to-do list before going on with the real living of life. That is not what my grandmother had in mind. I loved God, to be sure, but I wasn't really aware of His intense interest in me, or His intense interest in my knowing who He was.

I left home at eighteen-years old and moved to where I was not near any of my family members or any of the spiritual influences with which I grew up. I began to feel separated from God and wondered where He was and how I could get back to Him. I would find a Catholic church wherever I went, but I never felt truly satisfied with my side of the relationship. I began to realize that a relationship with God was what I wanted. Maybe it was because of being away from home, away from my family, and out on my own that I was subconsciously looking for family and wanted it from God Himself.

As I moved from place to place, I began meeting people who asked me if I had studied the Bible. I had not. Before then, I'd never read the actual Bible. I'd been exposed to scripture through mass which is a formal religious rite Catholics attend every Sunday. In the mass, no one takes out a Bible and reads it. There are Bible verses in the reader called the Missalette, but I never even knew these came from the Bible until I grew up, read the Bible, visited mass whenever I was home, and realized, "Oh, these are Bible verses."

Once I became an adult and wanted to have more of a relationship with God, I studied the Bible with various people from various denominations. I loved studying the Bible and loved being around people who were so interested. Still, I always felt like something was missing. Even though I studied with various people, I could never find a place I wanted to land until I found the church where I currently worship. It is non-denominational, which means it is not one of the branches of the Christian church affiliated with historical groups like Baptists, Church of God in Christ, Presbyterians, or those named after their originators, such as Martin Luther or John Wesley.

My current church is great for teaching me how to pray and how to read the Bible for myself so I can apply the truths of its pages to my life. It is also great for teaching me how to love and serve others in and outside of the church, how to allow others to be in my life, and how to deal with sin in not only my behaviors but in my heart—through repentance and confession. I've also learned a host of ways to be in community with people and with God.

Other than going to church every Sunday, I'd never seen or even thought of community as part of worship. I'd found a place to belong in a spiritual community, but something still felt like it was missing. In my own time, as I read the Bible, I began to get to know God on deeper and deeper levels. I even began to hear Him. Maybe *hear* isn't the right word: I began to intuit that He was speaking directly to me in the verses on the page and during contemplative times with Him in my heart. The

Bible wasn't just a list of do's and don'ts, or a bunch of stories on how to be spiritual. The Bible is a conduit, almost like a telephone line between the God of heaven and my heart.

I would try to have conversations with people about my experiences, but I received a variety of responses. Some people gave me deer-in-the-headlights stares. Others would reframe my experiences telling me what God actually meant or that the experience wasn't actually Him. Sometimes, the person would change the subject because they couldn't relate. One person actually told one of my family members, "Tracy is crazy," three times in one conversation. She wasn't talking about something I did or said; she was talking about an experience I'd shared with her. I learned I needed to be careful of the types of experiences I shared.

With the exception of a few people, it wasn't long before I began to feel there weren't many people I could talk to about what I was learning from God. My spiritual world consisted of daily prayers in the morning, quiet times either before or after those morning prayers, church service, a midweek church service, and a weekly Bible study group. I would participate in smaller, more intimate Bible study groups when someone wanted to get to know God on deeper levels. Then I'd go to weekly meetings with a *discipler*, someone older in the faith whose job was to help me learn how to follow God.

Even though I was heavily involved in these routines, I found that when I just sat and thought about God or pretended He was in the same room, I felt closest to Him. The first book that brought this idea to my mind was *Practicing His Presence* by Brother Lawrence. (1) Brother Lawrence chronicled his daily time in the Lord's presence and gave a great framework for praying without ceasing. I started practicing that and found some of the delight about which Brother Lawrence was speaking.

Soon after that, God introduced me to prayer retreats, which were weekend-long excursions I took once a year with other Christian therapists and psychologists. I began to learn more about the spiritual disciplines and a particular form of spiritual discipline called *contemplative prayer*. Differing from the kind of petition prayers with which most of the people I know are familiar, contemplative prayer has more to do with a sort of back-and-forth between the person in prayer and God. In this chapter, I would like to teach you three of the forms of contemplative prayer that have helped me not only grow closer to God, but to believe what He says in His Word.

The forms of contemplative prayer we will dive into are remembrance, lectio divinia, and centering prayer. I first learned about remembrance when the priest would quote Jesus in mass. He would quote Jesus saying, "Do this in remembrance of me." The other two, lectio divinia and Centering Prayer have been around for centuries in contemplative-prayer communities.

Remembrance

What is a Remembrance?

James 1:17 says, "Every good gift and every perfect gift is from above, coming down from the Father of lights" (ASV). The good in our life is from God. The purpose of remembrance is to reflect on what has been done and to cultivate a feeling of gratitude. When we revisit what someone has done, whether just in our thoughts or when we are recounting the event to another person, that same wave of gratitude washes over us again. Remembrance can be a form of contemplative prayer in that you take the time to think on the people, events, and blessings you have received from others.

Blessings come in all kinds of forms. They don't have to be in the form of an event or something we have received. A blessing can be a realization that dawns on us and brings an insight to our understanding or a smile to our face. Knowing that all good gifts are from above, even when the gift is from another human being, that relationship is a blessing from God, or the action that person chose to do is a blessing coming through them from above. The Holy Spirit prompted the giver and she listened. In this form of contemplation, we train ourselves to stop and think about the good in our lives. Framing it from James 1:17 helps us to train ourselves to know God. We can practice remembrance as a spiritual discipline with the intent of discovering who God really is.

When we hear a comment about someone we

know that doesn't fit what we have experienced of that person, some of us will verbally say something like, "That's not the Cindy I know." The rest of us, typically those more wary of confrontation, will at least think it. Even if we may not say anything to the person bringing the information for fear of confrontation, we mull over what we just heard against what we know of the person in question.

That's what we have to do with God and with ourselves. When an enemy voice whispers something about God, and we have developed our relationship with Him, our first inclination should be to assert, "That's not the Father I know." Although none of us can know all of who God is, we will be equipped enough with practice to know whether a report matches our experience.

The same thing is true concerning information about ourselves. When something is whispered to us about ourselves such as, "You're nothing; you're not good enough," remembrance as a spiritual discipline can help us become more familiar with how God sees us. We can respond or deflect that lie by recalling that we are His friends (John 15:15), we are precious and we are honored in His sight… because He loves us (Isaiah 43:4), and if we believe, we have the right to be His children (John 1:12). Remembrance in this manner helps us debunk negative thoughts we have about ourselves.

The following four steps are designed to take you through the process of engaging in remembrance:

1. Recall something, someone, or some event in your life for whom or for which you are genuinely grateful. The person or event does not have to be religious or spiritual, just something or someone that brought you genuine joy at some moment, or a memory that garners a visceral response of gratitude when you think on it. It could be an event, time spent with a loved one, an accomplishment, or time alone when you were able to refresh and recharge.

2. Next spend a few minutes recalling the memory, letting your mind see the scene as it occurred. When you are first learning this technique, set a timer. Recalling a memory can be likened to a form of time travel because it allows your heart to reexperience the joy or your body to reexperience the joyful sensations. Be there in your mind. Try to 5, 4, 3, 2, 1 (your five senses) the moment if you can:

    a. What are five things you saw in the place where you were?

    b. Can you name four things you heard?

    c. Can you recall three things you felt? Emotions?

    d. Can you recall two things you might have smelled?

    e. Can you recall one thing, if any, you tasted?

3. Journal as much of the experience as you can. Writing helps to solidify memories in the brain and in the heart.

4. Pray on your knees if you are alone and thank God for the person, thing, situation, or moment. Let Him know what you understand His role to have been in the remembrance.

Full Moon Rising

Here's a personal example of a remembrance of mine, so you'll see how remembrance prayer works. I'll title this remembrance: "Full Moon Rising."

I was on a prayer retreat after the end of a particularly arduous semester in graduate school with the group of Christian therapists and psychologists. One of the retreat coordinators was sharing a story of her and her sister's trip to Jerusalem. After a long day of touring, their group disbanded, and she and her sister heard that evening would have a full moon rising. They decided to go atop a hill known as a great vantage point for watching the moon rise over the land. She described the moon rise in all its majesty and wonder. I was transfixed listening to her account. I myself had never seen a full moon actually rising on the spot and wished I could experience it.

Just as I was thinking this, she mentioned that there was a full moon rising scheduled that evening, and maybe some of us would get to see it. I was in. I was hopeful.

Later, I went to my room to put on some comfortable shoes and grab a light sweater to head out to one of the gardens for some time alone with God. Although this was in summer, the retreat was located at a retreat center in Malibu, California, where the evenings can be a bit on the cool side. I found a trail that led down and around to the side of a hill. A little bench was built into the hillside. I sat down, wrapped my sweater around my shoulders, and bowed my head to say a little prayer of thanks for the retreat, the beautiful program presented, and nature all around. As my head bowed and eyes closed, I felt prompted to look up. It felt like a light hand was lifting my chin. As I lifted my bowed head and opened my eyes, the full moon was rising right there in front of me! I was about to miss it, but God allowed me to see it. He wanted me to see it. In my recalling of this remembrance using the 5, 4, 3, 2, 1 method:

5: I saw: the midnight blue sky (it wasn't midnight. I'm describing the color), clouds, the outline of the hillside, flowers along the side of the hill, and mountains in the distance.

4: I heard: nightlife: frogs chirping in a nearby fountain, the rustle of wind through the trees, the sound of an animal walking in the underbrush, and the ocean waves crashing far below in the distance.

3: I felt: gratitude for the experience, love because I believed God was answering the wish I had sitting in the workshop, and awe that He would take the time not only to bring me to this moment, but move me to lift my head and eyes so I did not miss it—My Full Moon Rising!

2: I smelled: the flowers along the hillside and the incense from inside the glass church on the hill below where I sat.

1: I tasted: the salt air from the ocean as well as the salt from the tears I was crying as I was witnessing the majesty of God in those few moments.

A remembrance involves your memory as well as your five senses. You don't have to call up as many as I did in this example, but it is helpful to engage as much of your memory as you can. Using your five senses helps to bring the gratitude back to life in real time, and it is a tangible way to connect with God during the remembrance.

<u>Why Remembrance is beneficial for your spiritual health and for tuning into the Savior's Voice.</u>

Think about it. Do we give good things to people we hate or people who mean nothing to us? We may if it's a task called for by our job. Or we may if doing so is the right thing to do, and we find ourselves in a position to do that right thing. There are times people do things for ulterior or selfish motives, but when we do things for people we love just for the sake of love, we give good things simply because we love them. If we are capable of that, how much more so is God? Remembrance helps us to recall who we are and whose we are. Who we are created to be is often a place of attack. Remembering goodness in our lives can be a powerful tool when dismantling negative ways of thinking.

Gaining a Different View

Earlier we discussed how *Cognitive Behavioral Therapy* is a form of treatment used to develop healthier thinking patterns. In a nutshell, patients are taught how to challenge unhelpful or negative thoughts with what is true or with what gives them an alternate perspective. CBT changes the person's cognitions or how they see themselves, others, and the world. Remembrance, practiced daily, gives them ample evidence to reframe how they think about themselves and helps them change how they think about God if they often call up examples of how He has shown up in their life.

Let's say another person experienced what I described above. Let's say she had a bad day at work and was taking a breather at the end of the day, outside, alone in nature, to contemplate the day. She has the choice when regaling that day to someone else to talk about the things at work that made it a bad day, or she can describe what she experienced at the end of the day out in nature as she was trying to decompress. The entirety of this book is about choosing—choosing what we think about and what we believe.

Lectio Divina

What is Lectio Divina?

Lectio Divina means divine reading—a way of reading the scriptures in a divinely inspired way. In other words, instead of just reading the verses on the page, we open ourselves up to what the Holy Spirit wants to teach us through that particular scripture, on that particular day, and for whatever particular season or situation in which we currently find ourselves.

<u>How do you engage with it and with God?</u>
There are five parts to Lectio Divina:

1. Reading
Choose a passage and read what it says in and of itself, just for content.

2. Meditate
Read that passage again and allow your mind and heart to be open to a word or phrase that sticks out to you. Meditate on that word or phrase. Meditate in this sense means keeping the word or phrase in your mind, thinking only of that word or phrase, repeating it silently, and not allowing other thoughts to interfere with or usurp that word or phrase. Ask God what He wants you to know or learn about this part of the passage as you turn it over and over in your mind.

While meditation is a decision on your part—something you set out to do—what happens during meditation is God's part. There is a phase during meditation where grace occurs. Grace is a gift from God to us. It can be a deeper or closer sense of His presence, a deeper understanding of the word or phrase on which you are meditating, or anything He wants for you in the moment. We can't make this connection with God happen. We simply look to

Him and have Him look at us. If He wants to take us to another level of prayer, He will, and if not, just sit in His presence. "Wait on the Lord," says Psalm 27:14 (KJV). The point is to let Him lead your mind and heart wherever He wants them to go. If He takes you further, you will receive insights into the scripture, your life, Him, and His relationship to you.

3. Journal

Write out what came to you. Where did you go during your time of meditation? What thoughts or memories came as you were sitting in God's presence? Did a situation come up, perhaps one you've been ignoring, that God wants you to attend to in some way? Continue listening for Him and see what comes through. Write it out.

4. Pray

To end the time of meditation, speak further with God about whatever has come to mind. Ask Him to show you something you need to know. He may be leading you to consider forgiveness, repentance, extension of grace, some kind of action, or more prayer, etc. It could be anything. Perhaps write out what comes to you in your conversation with God in dialogue form: what are you asking Him, and what is He answering. The more you do this, the more you will learn how to hear God's voice and follow his lead.

5. Action

Decide on something you can do or carry out based on your time of reading and sitting in God's presence. For example, based on your time of meditating, can you share the insight you've learned with someone? Can you blog about it? Is there someone in your life you can serve in a way that would be meaningful to them? Action—doing something for God or for others is an important step in solidifying the spiritual and mental health benefits Lectio Divina can provide.

Why is Lectio Divina beneficial for your spiritual health and for tuning into the Savior's voice?

Contemplative prayer is one of the spiritual disciplines that shapes your spirit. The spirit part of man is the part of his triune self—body, mind (or soul), and spirit—that is closest to God. Just as physical exercise benefits your body and intellectual exercise benefits your mind and by proxy, your emotions, spiritual exercise is beneficial for spirit formation. It is how one's spirit is stretched, purified, and matured. Spiritual formation aids in the transformation process of becoming more and more like Christ discussed in 2 Corinthians 3:18.

Centering Prayer

What is Centering Prayer?

Centering prayer is prayer that is centered entirely on the presence of God. A form of healing prayer, the essence of centering prayer is entering into God's presence and allowing Him to lead the process or do whatever He thinks needs to be done. God may want to provide an insight, bring healing, or have you let go of something you've held onto for too long. In God's presence, He may point out something that negatively impairs your mental health or something that stunts your spiritual growth and development.

There are seven steps to engaging in centering prayer with God:

> 1. Sit in a quiet place where you will not be disturbed.
> Take three deep breaths, close your eyes, then allow your breath to return to normal.
> 2. Choose a word of intention.
> This can be a phrase, but it's good to start with only a word at first, until you become more familiar with the discipline.
> 3. Say the prayer: "Lord Jesus, I consent to Your presence and to Your work in my life."
> 4. Sit in silence, keeping your mind on that word of intention.
> It's okay to start with as little as two to three minutes of silence with the intention of increasing your time to twenty minutes. Of course, you can remain in God's presence longer as you progress and become more comfortable with the process and with sitting still. God may show you what you need right away. But for the purpose of developing the skill, twenty minutes is the recommended amount of time because this is akin to doing cardio vascular exercise. It takes at least twenty minutes to raise the heart rate up to a point at which the body reaches a zone where the benefits are located. In centering

prayer, twenty minutes is the recommended amount of time for you to train yourself with being still and silent for the purpose of learning contemplative prayer.

5. Just Be.

Wait for the Lord to reveal what He wants to show you during this time. Let it unfold. You may receive a thought or an impression, or you may see what looks like a whole movie scene in your head. Just watch and be still. Know that you are safe in God's presence.

6. End with a prayer.

This can be in words or journaled out, but thank God for the time you spent, what He showed you, what you learned, and any healing you sensed.

7. Take three more deep breaths.

Open your eyes to end the practice.

Why is Centering Prayer beneficial for your spiritual health and for tuning into the Savior's voice.

As mentioned before, centering prayer can be a form of healing prayer. In reference to it, Jesus is known as the Divine Therapist. When people go to therapy, they sit with the therapist and choose what parts of their story they want to tell for the purpose of healing or making life and relational changes. The therapist helps clients to process the story, which helps to heal the pain and grief that are attached.

In centering prayer, once you close your eyes and enter into God's presence, and you consent to Christ's work in your life, at some point during the stillness, He (not you, as in therapy) will bring up a story He wants you to process. God may have you process a story or event you may have been shelving or out of fear. Often something is hindering your journey in some way. That thing is keeping you trapped and hampering your ability to grow and be who you are. You are being blocked from knowing who God really is. Unconscious pain gnaws on your heart. The Lord may bring that troubling thing to the surface, show you in some way that He's got your back, and assure you that despite the troubling thing, He has never left nor forsaken you. At other times, no story emerges. No memory pops up. You can experience a sense of God's presence that brings healing in and of itself.

The benefit of centering prayer is that it is often those very stories from our painful past that hinder our belief in God and in ourselves. In Chapter Two, I spoke about a process in the brain called imprinting where, until you are about twelve or thirteen years old, you take in information indiscriminately. In later years, when information enters, your brain will unconsciously look for a match. If there is one, you will take in the information as validation of an old belief. If there isn't a match, the brain usually doesn't have a problem rejecting it. Any healing that comes in centering prayer time in God's presence can aid you in believing what you know of God and rejecting what you know not to be true of God or of yourself.

Using the tools mentioned in this chapter is a good way to start honing your listening device – your heart – for the purpose of building what and who you will believe. In the final chapter, I will illustrate a life that is tuned into the Savior's voice.

Chapter Twelve
Illustration of A Life Tuned-In

Most mornings I wake up between 5 and 6 a.m. The first thing I have is a cool drink of water from the hydro flask next to my bed, and then I walk to the bathroom and flip on the lights to wake up. After refreshing myself, I go into my loft, which is an open space above my living and dining room areas. It's also my writing space. As I write this chapter, today is a nice, chilled, fall day—my favorite kind of morning. I turn on the electric fireplace, grab an Afghan blanket to snuggle down into my favorite chair, a recliner given to me by a pastor during a trying time in my life.

I drop a couple of drops of either orange or peppermint essential oils into my palm, close my eyes, and inhale a few deep, cleansing breaths of the essential oils to settle my heart and wake my mind. I reach for my Bible and my journal on the side table next to my chair and take a few moments to check in with the Holy Spirit to see if He will put anything on my heart for study this morning. I don't get a sense that anything is being presented, so I open my Bible and turn to Philippians 4:13. "I can do all things through Him who gives me strength" (NIV). I take a deep breath, pause, and read it again, "I can do everything through Christ who strengthens me." I decide to go back and read the opening to this section in Philippians four.

Beginning in verse 10, Paul is thanking the Philippians for the gifts they've provided, and he is discussing the knowledge he has of having much and having little. As Paul talks about the secret of contentment, on this particular morning I wonder: *What's that like? What is contentment?*

I decide to prayerfully engage verses 10-13, through Lectio Davina. I read the passage again, this time slowly, keeping my mind open and heart receptive to any word or phrase from the passage that stands out this morning. I land on the first part of verse 11 which says, "I am not saying this because I am in need" (NIV). I decide to sit with those ten words, mulling them over in my mind. I engage with the passage for a few moments by sitting silently thinking only of "I am not saying this because I am in need." I might ask the Holy Spirit something like: "Why is this passage coming to me right at this moment?" Then I pick up my journal and write the following:

This passage is coming

to me because I hope that this is where my life is at the moment: that anything I say, I say because it is true. Not because it may be something someone wants to hear. I truly believe what is coming out of my mouth because I know, and I know with certainty, that God has my back. I am free to engage with others because I am free to engage with me. I believe that I have learned, as Paul had, to be content in every (or at least most), situation(s). I am where I am either because of the choices I have made, or because God, through his setting up of divine appointments, has taken me to where I am at the moment. (I smile to myself as I realize it is probably both).

I also know both plenty and want, but I know what it is like to be content as well. Whatever happens, I trust and believe that Jesus will carry me through. Whether I am carried on the wings of success or through the valley of defeat, with the help of the Lord, I can get through to the other side. God has taken me through many a victory and many a trial. And though during both I have been tempted to think that I did it alone in victory or that I deserve defeat, I choose to believe that God has a plan for my life and that He works out all things for my good.

I may write a little more in my journal before closing it, but the gist of the writing and the prayer is that it flows from a heart that chooses to believe. The line that stood out did so because Jesus wanted to encourage me with what He thinks of my journey at this point in my life. I end the session by writing what is coming to my heart from the broadcast voice of the Savior. Contemplative prayer is effective in teaching you how to tune in to God's broadcast network.

I close my journal, say a little prayer, and return to my bedroom to get ready for the day. My time with the

Lord makes me feel suited and armored-up having spent time in prayer, in the Word, and having been reinforced by allowing myself to tune into the Savior's voice. In any given time of study, any of the voices can end up speaking into the life of the person. Here are examples of the broadcasts that could come through if it weren't for the fact that I was tuned into the Savior's voice.

> Self may have commented to me during the contemplation of the passage, "Why did you pick that line? It doesn't make sense that you would choose this line, or that the line would even stand out to you. You are always worried about one thing or another."

Or given aspects of my personal story, once this scripture came to mind, if I were tuned into the Self-voice, maybe I would have been plagued, even if unconsciously, with the thought or belief of being evil. The Self-voice would try to make me fear that somehow, I was still on the path of being evil; therefore, in some sort of spiritual danger if I was actually not feeling content. I would not have been able to bask in what the Savior's voice was broadcasting to my heart and mind. I may not have even landed on that portion of the scripture during that time of reading.

If I were tuned into Society's voice at the time,

maybe my thoughts would have gone here:

> Society may have commented to me: "You aren't in need? Of course, you are! You have to keep striving to make it! If you aren't meeting a need, how will you ever keep up with the Joneses?"

Society's voice keeps you looking to worldly desires and possessions as a means of being content. The problem with that is, when contentment comes from your possessions, you never have contentment because there are always more things to acquire. Think about it, how many people do you know who run out and get the latest iPhone or other gadget whenever there is an upgraded version? Is it that the version they have no longer works? The Society voice will have you buying the newest phone although the one you currently have is still working and may not even be paid for yet.

If I were tuned into Satan's broadcast, here is how it could have gone:

> Satan's voice may have stated, "You don't have time to be sitting in silence just thinking. Who do you think you are? You'll never have enough, you'll never be enough, you'll always have need. You're just a bottomless,

empty pit."

Thank goodness I wasn't listening to this voice that morning, right? Can you imagine how the rest of my day would have gone? Can you imagine what it probably went like having listened to the Savior voice? Let's have a look:

Emerging from my bedroom, I go to the kitchen for breakfast. I have a fleeting thought that I will be late for work, and then another in rapid succession that I am always late for work, and my day will be ruined because of it. Instead of rushing through the kitchen to grab a cup of coffee to go and a piece of half buttered toast, I take a deep breath, look at the clock on the stove, and tell myself that I have plenty of time. I remind myself that I gave myself enough margin by having a good night's sleep, waking up at my usual time, spending time with the Lord, and then getting dressed. I remind myself that I am not in fact going to be late, and I sit down to have a bowl of fruit and cottage cheese. I enjoy my coffee and toast and pour another cup of coffee into my tumbler, intending to take it with me.

That early negative thought about myself was not the last one that flitted through my mind that day, but I, through practice, have learned to turn down the voices that compete for my attention. As with the thought that: *I am always late*—it isn't true. I am almost never late for anything, but that doesn't stop the other voices—either from Self through self-condemnation, Satan through outright lies, or Society through comparison—from chiming in with material for me to stress over.

Over the course of my walk with the Lord, I have used all of the principles included here. I have learned to lean into God and turn up the volume on the Savior's voice. Except for times of extreme stress, I don't usually have the barrage of assaults that I had earlier in my Christian walk. When they do occur, I have tools in my arsenal to fight them rather than give in to them and allow them to define me.

I share this not to brag or insinuate that I have arrived. Our walk with the Savior is a lifelong journey. Much of what we learn can be applied with a little conscientiousness. We have to remember what we have learned. God is teaching us through people, situations, and circumstances all of the time.

One of my favorite stories in the Bible is of the Israelites walking through the Red Sea on dry ground to escape the Egyptians. Moments before doing this, they'd looked up to see that the Egyptians were coming after them. They'd followed Moses out of Egypt. He'd delivered them, by God's hand, out of slavery. The Egyptians changed their minds and decided to pursue the Israelites and take them back into captivity. The Israelites panicked and even said to Moses that they'd asked him to leave them alone, that they'd wanted to stay in Egypt to serve the Egyptians. Moses didn't panic. He stated my favorite line in all of the Bible, "Do not be afraid. Stand firm and you will see the deliverance the Lord will bring you today. The Egyptians you see today you will never see again. The Lord will fight for you; you need only to be still" (Exodus 14:13-14 [NIV]).

Deliverance from Egypt is our story too. From what do you need deliverance? Is it a certain mindset that keeps you stuck and unable to walk in all God has for you? Do you feel unable to be the person you were originally created to be? If you're a child of God, you have already received deliverance (Isaiah 53:5).

Although the Israelites' walking through the Red Sea is part of their history, it is part of ours too. That event stands as a metaphor for our deliverance. The Lord delivered us too, the moment we made our good confession. Whether we walk in that deliverance is entirely up to us. Walking out our freedom all starts and ends in the mind—what we let in, and how we think about what we have let in.

Being still is a good place to start to train yourself to walk in the deliverance Jesus gave. In the case of this book, walking in that deliverance means for you to choose whom you will believe. God split the sea so you could walk right through it. What is your sea? One of mine was the belief that I was made evil. Your sea is billowing before you, waiting to drown you in a lie. There may in fact be something you are facing that is as big as the sea to you, but God is bigger.

When the veil in the temple was torn at the moment of Christ's death, your sea was split, just as the Israelites' was. Walk through to the other side and live the life Jesus purchased for you. Stop allowing yourself to be debilitated by the background noise that constantly competes for your attention. Those voices aren't going anywhere until the end of this portion of human history. Those voices are part of the spiritual battle. The degree to which you allow them access to your thoughts and your choices is up to you.

I can't stress it enough. You have to choose. You have the power, given to you in the form of free will, to choose. In all that is going on, it may not seem you are powerful or free, but you are. You have been delivered. The Egyptians you saw earlier in your life, you need never see again. You need only to be still.

THE END

Endnotes

Chapter One
1. Tozer, A.W. Knowledge of The Holy: The Attributes of God: Their Meaning in Christian Life. Harrisburg, PA, Christian Publications, 1961.

Chapter Two
1. Ansa, Tina McElroy. Ugly Ways. Orlando, FL, Harcourt Brace & Co., 1993.
2. Information on imprinting: https://en.wikipedia.org/wiki/Imprinting_(psychology)
3. Information on Modeling: https://dictionary.apa.org/modeling-theory
https://courses.lumenlearning.com/suny-hccc-ss-151-1/chapter/observational-learning-modeling/

Chapter Three
1. Bunyan, John. The Pilgrim's Progress. New York, NY, G. H. McKibbin, 1899.
2. False Self: Dr. Donald Winnicott - https://depthcounseling.org/blog/winnicott-true-false-self
3. Erikson's stages of development: https://www.simplypsychology.org/Erik-Erikson.html
4. Differentiation: Bowen, Murry B - https://www.goodtherapy.org/blog/self-differentiation-why-it-matters-in-families-relationships-0831174
5. Intrapsychic differentiation: https://theallendercenter.org/2017/10/the-differentiated-self-healthy-relationship/
6. Allen, James, 1864-1912. As a Man Thinketh.

Mount Vernon, N.Y., Peter Pauper Press, 1951.
7. Scope of Practice definition:
http://archive.camft.org/COS/The_Therapist/Legal_Articles/Mary/Scope_of_Practice.aspx
8. Soul Wounds definition:
https://ct.counseling.org/2007/06/dignity-development-diversity-6/

Chapter Four
1. Charlton's Heston interview:
https://www.youtube.com/watch?v=otvt2IKJtJQ

2. Eldridge, John. Waking The Dead: The Glory of a Heart Fully Alive. Nashville, TN, Thomas Nelson Books, 2000.

Chapter Five
1. Orlowski, Jeff, dir The Social Dilemma. Exposure Labs, 2020. Netflix netflix.com/title/81254224

Chapter Six
1. Chinese Parable:
https://www.incendo-uk.com/leadership-lesson-chinese-farmer/
2. Thomas, Gary. Sacred Pathways: Discover Your Soul's Pathway to God. Grand Rapids, MI, Zondervan, 2000.

Chapter Eight

1. Relationship between neurobiology and shame: https://cptsdfoundation.org/2019/04/11/the-neuroscience-of-shame/

2. Pressfield, Steven. The War of Art: Break Through the Blocks and Win Your Inner Creative Battles. Chichester, England, Capstone Publishing, 2012.

Chapter Nine:

1. Gungor, Michael, Gungor, Lisa. You Make Beautiful Things Out of Us. Capital CMG Publishing, 2009.

2. Kondo, Marie and Emily Woo. Zeller, The Life-Changing Magic of Tidying Up: The Japanese Art of Decluttering and Organizing. [United States], Tantor Media, Inc, 2015.

Chapter Ten:

1. Mayer, John, Palladino, Pino. Stop This Train. BMG Bumblebee, 2006.

2. Missed Blessings Story: https://www.stpaulcumc.org/warehouse-of-blessings/

3. Lawrence, Francis. 2007. I Am Legend. United States: Warner Brothers

4. Hendrix, Jimi, Bold as Love. Track Records, UK, 1967.

Chapter Eleven:

1. Brother Lawrence, and Laubach, Frank. Practicing His Presence: One of the Greatest Pieces of Christian Literature of All Time. Jacksonville, FL,

SeedSowers, 1973.